September 1939, September 1945. Germany invades Poland, Japan at last surrenders in Tokyo Bay on board the battle cruiser USS *Missouri*. Two dates and two places at opposite ends of the earth, the beginning and the end of the century's most destructive war – with one notable factor in common, the aeroplane. Waves of bombers and fighters unleashed by Hitler on 1st September 1939 wrecked the entire Polish defence system in a few hours, and made the *Blitzkrieg* possible; and it was two American bombers on 6th and 9th August 1945, over Hiroshima and Nagasaki which brought the Japanese, still fighting on, to their knees and forced them to surrender seven days later. All through the intervening years of the war, too, the role of the aeroplane had been absolutely crucial. Its influence had been decisive at the war's major turning points: in Europe, first in the Battle of Britain, then in the strategic bombing of Germany and again in Allied landings in Normandy. In the Pacific there had been the Japanese attack on Pearl Harbor, then the Battle of Midway and other great air-sea battles, and later on the American bombardment of Japan. After twenty years the predictions of Giulio Douhet and William Mitchell were indeed vindicated.

Exactly as had happened in the First World War, this war proved to be a powerful stimulus for the development of aviation. Between 1939 and 1945 the aeroplane evolved beyond recognition from its prewar form. The best piston-engine fighters flew at speeds of about 470 mph (750 km/h), almost double that of the last biplanes; the most advanced bomber put into service, the American B-29, operated at such high altitude and speed and had such powerful defensive armament that it was practically immune from any attack. Great strides had been made in the introduction of new materials, and after a full development of the piston engine came at last the jet.

Now industry was to play an even greater part in the conduct of war than it had in the First World War, and it grew rapidly to meet the demand. The Second World War was won by those countries which had better resources than the others and were able to make the best use of them. It was the time when the great strength of the United States first showed itself in world affairs.

At the outbreak of war in Europe, American military aviation was unprepared, especially as regards the quality of its aircraft. The industry had simply not received sufficient encouragement to plan for really large scale production runs. Then a new impetus came in September 1939 with the repeal of the Neutrality Act of 1935 which had prohibited the export of military supplies; a "cash and carry" principle was established for arms sales. The aircraft industry quickly received encouragement in the form of military orders from France and Britain. In March 1941 the Lend-Lease Act was passed – a matter of sheer necessity in view of the plight of Britain and France – and then America's industries went into overdrive. In the two years preceding entry into the war America produced 6,028 aircraft in 1940 and 19,445 in 1941. The great majority of these went to bring the air forces of the army and the navy up to strength: in 1939 the

USAAC had 2,400 aircraft of all types and the US Navy had 2,500, of which 600 were carrier-based; in December 1941 these figures had risen to 3,305 combat-ready aircraft for the army and about 3,300 for the navy. In the June of 1941, as a further measure of reorganisation, the USAAC was given its own general staff, made into a separate service and called the US Army Air Force (USAAF).

In spite of these steps, however, the United States was caught completely unawares by the Japanese when, on the morning of 7th December 1941, they attacked Pearl Harbor. Argument continues as to why the United States was taken by surprise, whether the reasons were political, diplomatic or purely military; but the most likely of them all was the fixed belief on the part of the Supreme Command that Japan was not an enemy to be feared, especially in the air. Pearl Harbor came as a nasty shock and set in train the most remarkable increase in the level of activity, which was already going at high speed. Not only did the American aircraft industry re-equip the USAAF and the US Navy with ever-increasing numbers of aeroplanes, but a great part of its production was also exported to Allied countries, mainly Britain and the USSR. The numbers tell the story: in 1942, a total of 47,836 aircraft were constructed (including 10,769 fighters and 12,627 bombers, of which 2,615 were four-engine and 7,247 twin-engine machines); in 1943 the total was 85,898 (including 23,988 fighters and 29,355 bombers, of which 9,615 were four-engine and 10,361 twin-engine); the peak was reached in 1944: 96,318 aircraft (including 38,873 fighters and 35,003 bombers, out of which 16,331 were four-engine machines and 10,058 twin-engine); finally, in the last year of the war 47,714 aeroplanes left the assembly lines, of which 21,696 were fighters and 16,492 bombers (6,865 four-engine and 4,454 twin-engine). The total number of combat aircraft built from 1941 to 1945 was 297,199: 99,742 fighters and 97,592 bombers – 35,743 of which were four-engine machines and 35,369 twin-engine.

The enormous growth in the volume of manufacturing was accompanied by a corresponding improvement in quality: the two air forces were able to field considerably better aircraft than most enemy air forces, whether in Europe or in the Pacific. On 1st January 1945 the United States had a total of 86,000 aircraft. Personnel had risen from 100,000 on 8th December 1941 to over a million in the following year and reached its highest total of 2,300,000 in 1943.

America's closes ally – politically as well as geographically – was Britain. On 3rd September 1939 the British had declared war on Germany. The Royal Air Force was undoubtedly the best able to face the air power of its adversary. As at 16th October 1939, as we are told in Sir Winston Churchill's memoirs, there were 1,500 combat-ready planes stationed throughout the British Isles and to these should be added an equal number in reserve; production had from May onwards reached a monthly total of 700 aircraft. The standard of the aircraft in service was, in the main, comparable with that of the *Luftwaffe*. The Battle of Britain, which lasted from 10th July (in all British records) to 31st October

1940, was the first great air battle of the Second World War. It was also the British aircraft industry's greatest trial of strength. All of Britain's resources, productive capacity and ability faced a life-and-death test before an audience on the ground whose whole future depended on the outcome, and whose gratitude went out to the defending airmen. For the enemy, it was the very first setback that fascism had encountered.

With the threat of invasion staved off, the British were able to organise a large increase in aircraft production. It was at this time the most famous aircraft of the RAF took to the air, amongst them the best versions of the Spitfire and the Mosquito; the heavy strategic bombers such as the Halifax and the Lancaster which were to be so effective in the destruction of the Third Reich's war machine. The first steps were taken in pursuit of a new ambitious objective: the creation of a jet-engine combat aircraft. Even though the Meteor only went into service in the last months of the war and although it was preceded by the German Me.262, Britain had the distinction of being the only Allied nation to achieve this during the war.

The aircraft industry notched up impressive annual production totals: 15,000 aircraft in 1940, 20,100 in 1941, 23,671 in 1942, 26,263 in 1943, 29,220 in 1944. At the end of the war the total number of aircraft of all types to be built had reached 125,254.

Whilst the RAF had the lion's share of this expansion, the strengthening of the Fleet Air Arm came about more slowly. In September 1939 (the Fleet Air Arm had become a separate service in May of that year) only 340 aircraft were in the service, 225 of which were carrier-based and generally inferior to those of the RAF. The Fleet Air Arm had to wait until 1942 for its modernisation to get under way with the first models of the Sea Hurricane and the Seafire. Subsequently, with the arrival of the most effective American aircraft, numbers were also greatly increased. In August 1945 the Fleet Air Arm had 1,300 planes in the front line out of an overall total of 11,500 aircraft.

The last great power to join the allied fight against the Third Reich was the Soviet Union. The pact with Germany, signed on 23rd August 1939, had last for only two years when, on 22nd June 1941, Hitler launched Operation Barbarossa. Initial German successes outstripped all predictions and, once again, this was due to air power: in the first nine hours of the invasion the *Luftwaffe* virtually wiped out the Soviet air forces, destroying 1,200 aircraft, 800 of them on the ground. Apart from the surprise factor (Hitler had issued no ultimatum before the onslaught) this staggering aggressive success was mainly due to the inferiority of Soviet aircraft; many front line aircraft had been made as far back as the mid 1930s.

Only at the beginning of 1942 did the USSR recover from this crushing blow when, having rebuilt her aircraft industry, she started to manufacture more up-to-date aircraft and to step up the tempo of production. A major contribution was also made by United States and British industry supplying the Soviet Union's armed forces. In all, from 1942 to 1944 no fewer than 14,833 aircraft of every type reached the Soviet Union. Among these were high-quality aeroplanes such as the British Hurricane and Spitfire fighters and the American P-47 Thunderbolt fighter and B-25 and A-20 medium bombers. Soviet designers before long managed to make up for lost time and produced excellent combat aircraft which in many ways were superior to those of the opposing forces: the Petlyakov Pe-2 bomber, the Ilyushin Il-2 and Il-10 close support and attack planes, the Yakovlev Yak-3 and Yak-9 and the Lavochkin La-5 and La-7 fighters. Production for the army air force and for the navy's air force rose from 8,000 aircraft in 1942 to 18,000 and 30,000 in 1943 and 1944, reaching 25,000 in the remaining months of the war in 1945.

France's role as an air power only survived the brief space of ten months, from 3rd September 1939 when, together with Britain, she declared war on Germany, until 22nd June 1940 when the Armistice was signed. At the outbreak of war the *Armée de l'Air* had a total of 1,400 combat-ready aircraft but of these almost two-thirds were obsolete. This was the price France had to pay for the lack of priority given to air defence, and consequent delays in reorganising the aircraft industry to prepare it for its necessary task. As the war began to take its course the supply of aircraft improved somewhat but not significantly. Although recourse was had to foreign aircraft to gain time and in spite of some really effective fighters coming into service (such as the Morane-Saulnier M.S.406 and, in very small numbers, the Dewoitine D.520) only 1,501 modern aircraft were in service on 10th May 1940, of which 784 were fighters. The *Armée de l'Air* fought valiantly but there was little it could do; on 14th June German troops entered Paris and eight days later the Armistice was signed.

And then there was the mighty neighbour, Germany, armed to the teeth from the start. When Hitler lit the fuse of war on 1st September 1939, he had the most powerful air force in the world and it was hardened from combat experience in Spain, where the civil war had ended only six months previously. The *Luftwaffe* had 4,840 front-line aircraft including 1,750 bombers and 1,200 fighters. This force was kept up to strength by an aircraft industry which was already producing 1,000 planes a month and which in 1939 was to produce no less than 8,300 aircraft of all types. Success followed on success: after Poland came Denmark and Norway, then the Netherlands, Belgium, Luxembourg and finally France. Only at the shores of the English Channel did the *Blitzkrieg* halt.

The Battle of Britain revealed a weakness in the theoretical basis of German military planning. The essence of German air planning at that time, unquestioned after its successful application in Spain, consisted of the use of medium day-time bombers as the main strategic weapon, and ground attack aircraft as the main tactical weapon.

Three-and-a-half months of air warfare against Britain showed that what had applied in the Spanish Civil War was quite inappropriate against a technically well equipped enemy, in quite a different kind of war. Facing a determined stand by the RAF, the He.III and Do.17 bombers lacked adequate defensive armament and what they had was of limited range. This made it necessary for the escorting Bf.109 fighters to stay in close formation with the bombers, who needed their constant protection; the fighters were thus unable to carry out any wider manoeuvres and so they could not serve with their full effectiveness. In addition, the Ju.87 Stuka, which had spread so much terror in Poland, Belgium and France, was completely at the mercy of the Spitfires and Hurricanes. The *Luftwaffe* lacked a heavy bomber, too, but in spite of the lessons of war Germany never equipped itself with an effective plane in this category.

Whatever their weaknesses, the Germans did continue to manufacture enormous quantities of aircraft, and adapted their designs all the time. Serving as it was on fronts half way round the world, the *Luftwaffe* could only achieve what it did with the backing of a vast industry which kept up very high levels of production throughout the Allied bombardments and in the face of shortages of strategic materials and fuel in the last years of the war. In 1940 10,800 aircraft of all types were constructed; 11,800 in the following year; 15,600 in 1942; 25,500 in 1943 and 39,800 in 1944; 8,000 aircraft were constructed in the first five months of 1945. Under the noses of its enemies Germany managed to become the first nation in the world to build and put into service a jet fighter aircraft. The Messerschmitt Me.262 made its appearance in the second half of 1944, followed shortly afterwards by the Arado Ar.234 and in the last months of the fighting by the Heinkel He.162.

Japan's experience was similar but compressed into three years and eight months of war. On the outbreak of war in the Pacific the Japanese air forces were of a very high standard and, above all, their potential was almost unknown to the Western powers. On 7th December 1941, the date of Pearl Harbor, the Imperial Army Air Force comprised approximately 1,500 combat-ready aircraft, whilst the navy's air force had about 1,400 aircraft. The naval air force was entrusted with the task of neutralising the US fleet, which it was to achieve with its carried-based units, while its land-based aircraft were used in a supporting role in the invasion of the Pacific islands. Most Japanese aircraft were of modern design; and they were flown by pilots and crews of fanatical enthusiasm and determination. After their initial ferocious success momentum was sustained until the second half of 1942, with their enemies in disarray. Air supremacy was lost, first by the navy's air force in the great air-sea battles of 1942, then by the army's air force as the sheer numbers of Japan's enemies, in the lengthening war, began to have their effect.

After this turning point the Japanese had to sustain a defensive war in which they were gradually driven back inside their sphere of expansion until they were reduced to fighting for the survival of their own homeland. Right up to the very end, however, the effort they put up was massive. After a total production of 4,768 aircraft in 1940, 5,088 were built in 1941 (of which 1,080 were fighters and 1,461 bombers); this rose to 8,861 in 1942 (2,935 fighters and 2,433 bombers); 16,693 in 1943 (7,147 fighters and 4,189 bombers); 28,180 in 1944 (13,811 fighters and 4,189 bombers); in the eight months left of the war in 1945 the assembly lines turned out 11,066 combat planes of which 5,474 were fighters and 1,934 were bombers. The greatest losses of aircraft were sustained in the desperate attempt to defend Japan from American raids and in the suicide missions of the last months of the war.

Italy was the third Axis power, without doubt the weakest and least prepared to contend with the strain of the war. On 10th June 1940, when Italy entered the war, joining Germany against France and Britain, the *Regia Aeronautica* had 3,296 aircraft distributed over Italy, the Aegean and Libya. Only just over half of these, however, could be considered combat-ready and numbered 1,796 comprising 783 bombers, 594 fighters, 268 spotter planes and 151 reconnaissance planes. It was still a force to be reckoned with in numbers but in quality it left much to be desired. This was not considered to be of great consequence by the highest generals, one of whom declared that "Italy would need several thousand dead before she sat down at the negotiating table".

Never was prophecy proved to be more false. From its unsuccessful operations in France onwards, the full extent of the *Regia Aeronautica*'s inadequacies was clearly revealed. Then the failed Italian missions in the Battle of Britain undertaken by the *Corpo Aereo Italiano* were even more conclusive. Handicapped by an inefficient industry, Italy was foundering in the midst of a war with enemies attacking on all sides. Mussolini and his ministers were under severe pressure, but help came from the Germans, who supplied the engines vitally needed by the Italian aircraft industry to build modern and powerful aircraft. The recovery benefited the fighter most of all, leading to the appearance of some Italian aircraft which could really contend with the opposition.

On the production front, however, success still eluded Italian aircraft manufacturers and this proved to be the weakness of the whole policy of war. Aggressive plans were no more than a waste of breath, and the war itself was a waste of lives. In 1940 a total of 3,257 aircraft were built; 3,503 in 1941; 2,818 in 1942 and 1,930 in the first eight months of 1943. On 8th September 1943 only 887 Italian aircraft were left.

After that date the toll was even heavier; Italy was divided and Italian airmen fought for opposing sides. In the south the airmen of the Balkan Air Force managed to reach the Allies and join them, and then continued to give their lives until the last day of the war. In the north, those who had chosen to cling to the German cause perished with the air force of the *Repúbblica Sociale Italiana*, trying to stem the irresistible tide of the American and British bombers.

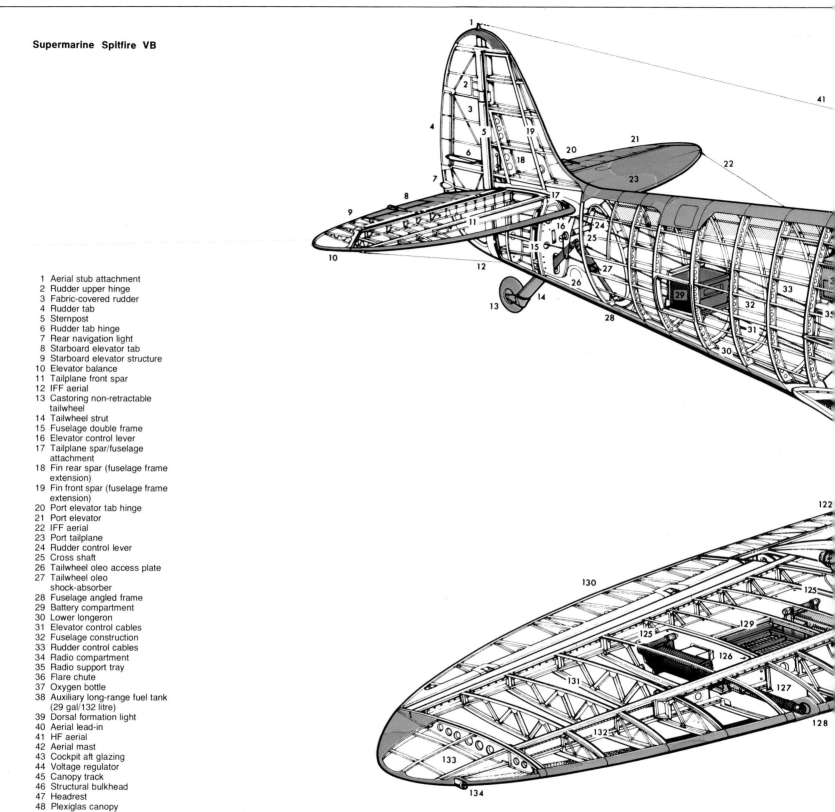

Supermarine Spitfire VB

1 Aerial stub attachment
2 Rudder upper hinge
3 Fabric-covered rudder
4 Rudder tab
5 Sternpost
6 Rudder tab hinge
7 Rear navigation light
8 Starboard elevator tab
9 Starboard elevator structure
10 Elevator balance
11 Tailplane front spar
12 IFF aerial
13 Castoring non-retractable tailwheel
14 Tailwheel strut
15 Fuselage double frame
16 Elevator control lever
17 Tailplane spar/fuselage attachment
18 Fin rear spar (fuselage frame extension)
19 Fin front spar (fuselage frame extension)
20 Port elevator tab hinge
21 Port elevator
22 IFF aerial
23 Port tailplane
24 Rudder control lever
25 Cross shaft
26 Tailwheel oleo access plate
27 Tailwheel oleo shock-absorber
28 Fuselage angled frame
29 Battery compartment
30 Lower longeron
31 Elevator control cables
32 Fuselage construction
33 Rudder control cables
34 Radio compartment
35 Radio support tray
36 Flare chute
37 Oxygen bottle
38 Auxiliary long-range fuel tank (29 gal/132 litre)
39 Dorsal formation light
40 Aerial lead-in
41 HF aerial
42 Aerial mast
43 Cockpit aft glazing
44 Voltage regulator
45 Canopy track
46 Structural bulkhead
47 Headrest
48 Plexiglas canopy
49 Rear-view mirror
50 Entry flap (port)
51 Air bottles (alternative rear fuselage stowage)
52 Sutton harness
53 Pilot's seat (moulded Bakelite)
54 Datum longeron
55 Seat support frame
56 Wingroot fillet
57 Seat adjustment lever
58 Rudder pedal frame
59 Elevator control connecting tube
60 Control column spade grip
61 Trim wheel

62 Reflector gunsight
63 External windscreen armour
64 Instrument panel
65 Main fuselage fuel tank (48 gal/218 litre)
66 Fuel tank/longeron attachment fittings
67 Rudder pedals
68 Rudder bar
69 King post
70 Fuselage lower fuel tank (37 gal/168 litre)
71 Firewall/bulkhead

72 Engine bearer attachment
73 Steel tube bearers
74 Magneto
75 "Fishtail"/exhaust manifold
76 Gun heating "intensifier"
77 Hydraulic tank
78 Fuel filler cap
79 Air compressor intake
80 Air compressor
81 Rolls-Royce Merlin 45 engine
82 Coolant piping
83 Port cannon wing fairing
84 Flaps

85 Aileron control cables
86 Aileron push tube
87 Bellcrank
88 Aileron hinge
89 Port aileron
90 Machine gun access panels
91 Port wingtip
92 Port navigation light
93 Leading-edge skinning
94 Machine gun ports (protected)
95 20mm cannon muzzle
96 Three-blade constant-speed propeller

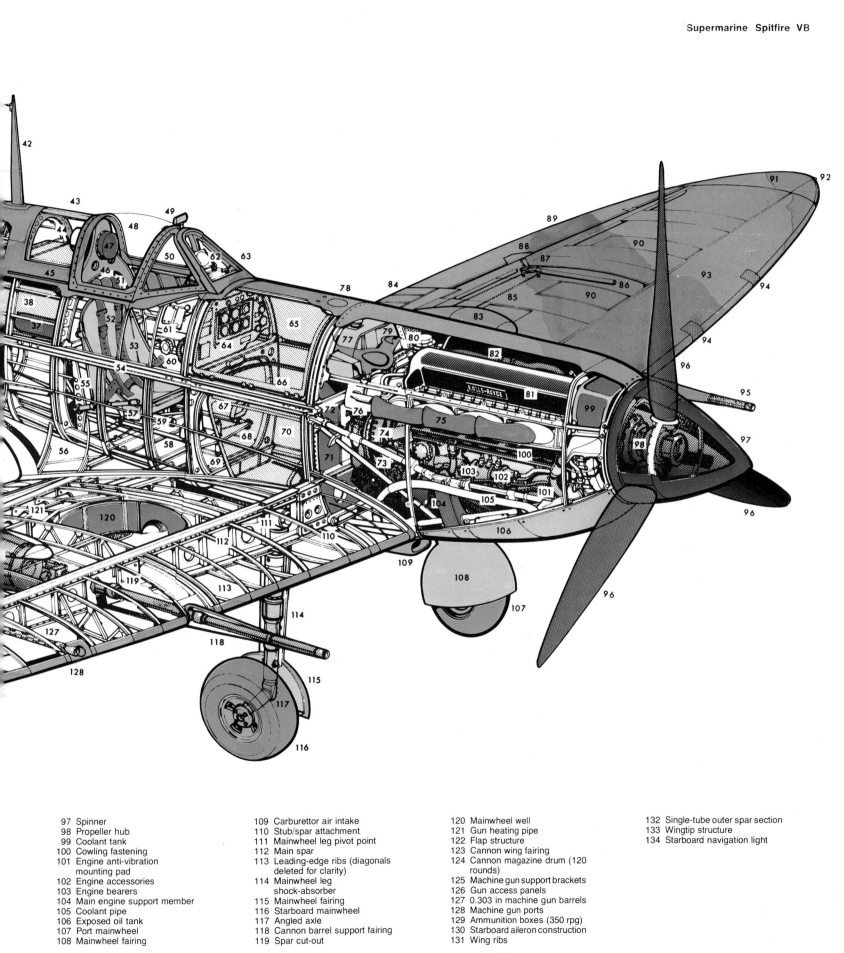

97 Spinner
98 Propeller hub
99 Coolant tank
100 Cowling fastening
101 Engine anti-vibration
    mounting pad
102 Engine accessories
103 Engine bearers
104 Main engine support member
105 Coolant pipe
106 Exposed oil tank
107 Port mainwheel
108 Mainwheel fairing

109 Carburettor air intake
110 Stub/spar attachment
111 Mainwheel leg pivot point
112 Main spar
113 Leading-edge ribs (diagonals
    deleted for clarity)
114 Mainwheel leg
    shock-absorber
115 Mainwheel fairing
116 Starboard mainwheel
117 Angled axle
118 Cannon barrel support fairing
119 Spar cut-out

120 Mainwheel well
121 Gun heating pipe
122 Flap structure
123 Cannon wing fairing
124 Cannon magazine drum (120
    rounds)
125 Machine gun support brackets
126 Gun access panels
127 0.303 in machine gun barrels
128 Machine gun ports
129 Ammunition boxes (350 rpg)
130 Starboard aileron construction
131 Wing ribs

132 Single-tube outer spar section
133 Wingtip structure
134 Starboard navigation light

Entry into service of the most important fighters of the Second World War

1937	1938	1939	1940	1941
Gloster Gladiator (GB)	Supermarine Spitfire (GB)	Messerschmitt Bf.109 (G)	Bristol Beaufighter (GB)	Focke Wulf Fw.190 (G)
Hawker Hurricane (GB)		Fiat C.R.42 (I)	Dewoitine D.520 (F)	Macchi M.C.202 (I)
Polikarpov I-16 (USSR)		Messerschmitt Bf.110 (G)	Grumman F4F Wildcat (USA)	Bell P-39 Airacobra (USA)
		Macchi M.C.200 (I)	Nakajima Ki-43 Hayabusa (J)	Curtiss P-40 Warhawk (USA)
		Nakajima Ki-27 (J)	Mitsubishi A6M Reisen (J)	Mikoyan-Gurevich MiG-3 (USSR)
				Lavochkin LaGG-3 (USSR)

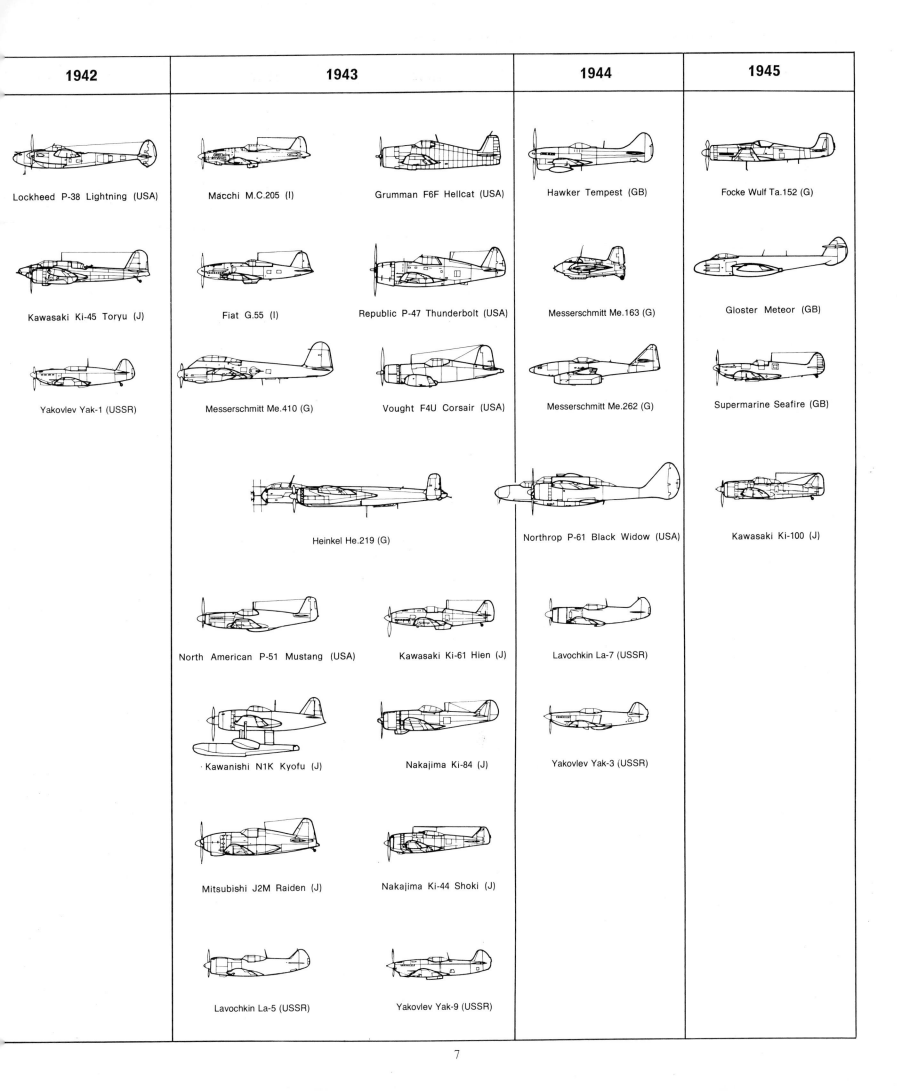

1942	1943	1944	1945
Lockheed P-38 Lightning (USA)	Macchi M.C.205 (I) / Grumman F6F Hellcat (USA)	Hawker Tempest (GB)	Focke Wulf Ta.152 (G)
Kawasaki Ki-45 Toryu (J)	Fiat G.55 (I) / Republic P-47 Thunderbolt (USA)	Messerschmitt Me.163 (G)	Gloster Meteor (GB)
Yakovlev Yak-1 (USSR)	Messerschmitt Me.410 (G) / Vought F4U Corsair (USA)	Messerschmitt Me.262 (G)	Supermarine Seafire (GB)
	Heinkel He.219 (G)	Northrop P-61 Black Widow (USA)	Kawasaki Ki-100 (J)
	North American P-51 Mustang (USA) / Kawasaki Ki-61 Hien (J)	Lavochkin La-7 (USSR)	
	Kawanishi N1K Kyofu (J) / Nakajima Ki-84 (J)	Yakovlev Yak-3 (USSR)	
	Mitsubishi J2M Raiden (J) / Nakajima Ki-44 Shoki (J)		
	Lavochkin La-5 (USSR) / Yakovlev Yak-9 (USSR)		

French fighters: 1938–39

MORANE-SAULNIER 406
Nation: France; *manufacturer:* SNCAO; *type:* fighter; *year:* 1938; *engine:* Hispano-Suiza 12 Y 12-cylinder V liquid-cooled, 860 hp; *wingspan:* 34 ft 10 in (10.65 m); *length:* 26 ft 9 in (8.15 m); *height:* 9 ft 3 in (2.82 m); *weight:* 6,000 lb (2,720 kg) (loaded); *maximum speed:* 302 mph (486 km/h) at 16,400 ft (5,000 m); *ceiling:* 30,840 ft (9,400 m); *range:* 497 miles (800 km); *armament:* 1 × 20 mm gun; 2 machine guns; *crew:* 1

POTEZ 630
Nation: France; *manufacturer:* SNCAN; *type:* fighter; *year:* 1938; *engine:* two Hispano-Suiza 14 Hbs 14-cylinder radial air-cooled, 640 hp each; *wingspan:* 52 ft 6 in (16.00 m); *length:* 36 ft 4 in (11.07 m); *height:* 11 ft 10½ in (3.61 m); *weight:* 8,488 lb (3,845 kg) (loaded); *maximum speed:* 280 mph (450 km/h) at 13,120 ft (4,000 m); *ceiling:* 32,800 ft (10,000 m); *range:* 760 miles (1,225 km); *armament:* 2 × 20 mm cannon; 1 machine gun; *crew:* 3

BLOCH 152
Nation: France; *manufacturer:* SNCASO; *type:* fighter; *year:* 1939; *engine:* Gnome-Rhône 14N 14-cylinder radial air-cooled, 1,060 hp; *wingspan:* 34 ft 7 in (10.54 m); *length:* 29 ft 10 in (9.10 m); *height:* 12 ft 11 in (3.95 m); *weight:* 5,908 lb (2,676 kg) (loaded); *maximum speed:* 320 mph (515 km/h) at 13,120 ft (4,000 m); *ceiling:* 32,800 ft (10,000 m); *range:* 373 miles (600 km); *armament:* 4 machine guns; *crew:* 1

CAUDRON C. 714
Nation: France; *manufacturer:* Caudron; *type:* fighter; *year:* 1939; *engine:* Renault 12 RO-3 12-cylinder V air-cooled, 450 hp; *wingspan:* 29 ft 5 in (8.96 m); *length:* 27 ft 11 in (8.50 m); *height:* 9 ft 5 in (2.87 m); *weight:* 3,858 lb (1,748 kg) (loaded); *maximum speed:* 303 mph (487 km/h) at 13,120 ft (4,000 m); *ceiling:* 30,000 ft (9,100 m); *range:* 559 miles (900 km); *armament:* 4 machine guns; *crew:* 1

HANRIOT NC 600
Nation: France; *manufacturer:* SNCAC; *type:* fighter; *year:* 1939; *engine:* two Gnome-Rhône MO/01 14 cylinder radial air-cooled, 700 hp each; *wingspan:* 41 ft 11 in (12.77 m); *length:* 28 ft 10½ in (8.78 m); *height:* 10 ft 3 in (3.12 m); *weight:* 8,818 lb (3,995 kg) (loaded); *maximum speed:* 337 mph (542 km/h) at 16,400 ft (5,000 m); *ceiling:* 26,250 ft (8,000 m); *range:* 534 miles (860 km); *armament:* 3 × 20 mm guns; 2 machine guns; *crew:* 2

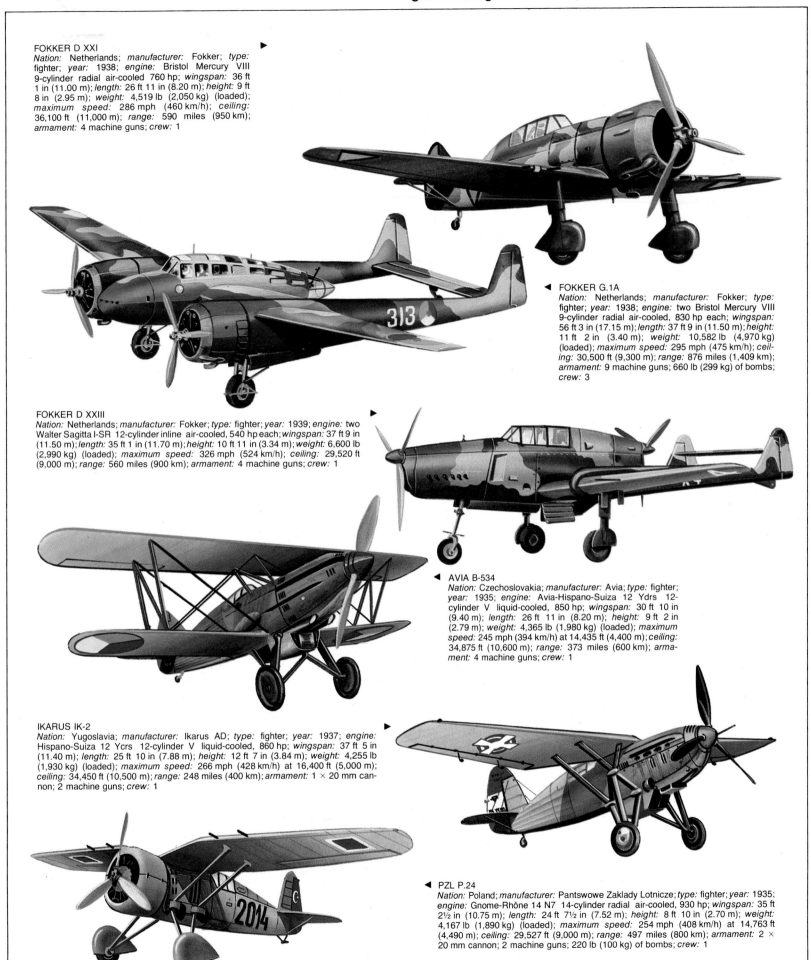

FOKKER D XXI
Nation: Netherlands; *manufacturer:* Fokker; *type:* fighter; *year:* 1938; *engine:* Bristol Mercury VIII 9-cylinder radial air-cooled 760 hp; *wingspan:* 36 ft 1 in (11.00 m); *length:* 26 ft 11 in (8.20 m); *height:* 9 ft 8 in (2.95 m); *weight:* 4,519 lb (2,050 kg) (loaded); *maximum speed:* 286 mph (460 km/h); *ceiling:* 36,100 ft (11,000 m); *range:* 590 miles (950 km); *armament:* 4 machine guns; *crew:* 1

FOKKER G.1A
Nation: Netherlands; *manufacturer:* Fokker; *type:* fighter; *year:* 1938; *engine:* two Bristol Mercury VIII 9-cylinder radial air-cooled, 830 hp each; *wingspan:* 56 ft 3 in (17.15 m); *length:* 37 ft 9 in (11.50 m); *height:* 11 ft 2 in (3.40 m); *weight:* 10,582 lb (4,970 kg) (loaded); *maximum speed:* 295 mph (475 km/h); *ceiling:* 30,500 ft (9,300 m); *range:* 876 miles (1,409 km); *armament:* 9 machine guns; 660 lb (299 kg) of bombs; *crew:* 3

FOKKER D XXIII
Nation: Netherlands; *manufacturer:* Fokker; *type:* fighter; *year:* 1939; *engine:* two Walter Sagitta I-SR 12-cylinder inline air-cooled, 540 hp each; *wingspan:* 37 ft 9 in (11.50 m); *length:* 35 ft 1 in (11.70 m); *height:* 10 ft 11 in (3.34 m); *weight:* 6,600 lb (2,990 kg) (loaded); *maximum speed:* 326 mph (524 km/h); *ceiling:* 29,520 ft (9,000 m); *range:* 560 miles (900 km); *armament:* 4 machine guns; *crew:* 1

AVIA B-534
Nation: Czechoslovakia; *manufacturer:* Avia; *type:* fighter; *year:* 1935; *engine:* Avia-Hispano-Suiza 12 Ydrs 12-cylinder V liquid-cooled, 850 hp; *wingspan:* 30 ft 10 in (9.40 m); *length:* 26 ft 11 in (8.20 m); *height:* 9 ft 2 in (2.79 m); *weight:* 4,365 lb (1,980 kg) (loaded); *maximum speed:* 245 mph (394 km/h) at 14,435 ft (4,400 m); *ceiling:* 34,875 ft (10,600 m); *range:* 373 miles (600 km); *armament:* 4 machine guns; *crew:* 1

IKARUS IK-2
Nation: Yugoslavia; *manufacturer:* Ikarus AD; *type:* fighter; *year:* 1937; *engine:* Hispano-Suiza 12 Ycrs 12-cylinder V liquid-cooled, 860 hp; *wingspan:* 37 ft 5 in (11.40 m); *length:* 25 ft 10 in (7.88 m); *height:* 12 ft 7 in (3.84 m); *weight:* 4,255 lb (1,930 kg) (loaded); *maximum speed:* 266 mph (428 km/h) at 16,400 ft (5,000 m); *ceiling:* 34,450 ft (10,500 m); *range:* 248 miles (400 km); *armament:* 1 × 20 mm cannon; 2 machine guns; *crew:* 1

PZL P.24
Nation: Poland; *manufacturer:* Pantswowe Zaklady Lotnicze; *type:* fighter; *year:* 1935; *engine:* Gnome-Rhône 14 N7 14-cylinder radial air-cooled, 930 hp; *wingspan:* 35 ft 2½ in (10.75 m); *length:* 24 ft 7½ in (7.52 m); *height:* 8 ft 10 in (2.70 m); *weight:* 4,167 lb (1,890 kg) (loaded); *maximum speed:* 254 mph (408 km/h) at 14,763 ft (4,490 m); *ceiling:* 29,527 ft (9,000 m); *range:* 497 miles (800 km); *armament:* 2 × 20 mm cannon; 2 machine guns; 220 lb (100 kg) of bombs; *crew:* 1

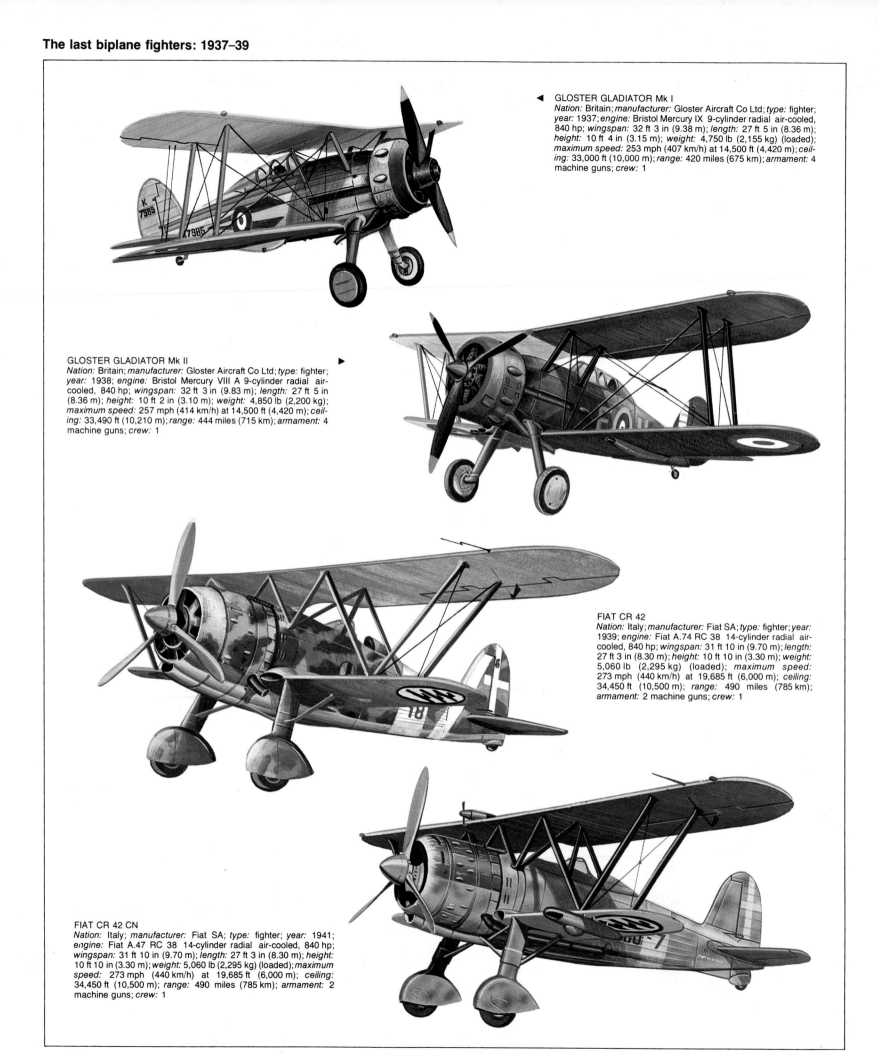

GLOSTER GLADIATOR Mk I
Nation: Britain; *manufacturer:* Gloster Aircraft Co Ltd; *type:* fighter;
year: 1937; *engine:* Bristol Mercury IX 9-cylinder radial air-cooled,
840 hp; *wingspan:* 32 ft 3 in (9.38 m); *length:* 27 ft 5 in (8.36 m);
height: 10 ft 4 in (3.15 m); *weight:* 4,750 lb (2,155 kg) (loaded);
maximum speed: 253 mph (407 km/h) at 14,500 ft (4,420 ft); *ceiling:* 33,000 ft (10,000 m); *range:* 420 miles (675 km); *armament:* 4
machine guns; *crew:* 1

GLOSTER GLADIATOR Mk II
Nation: Britain; *manufacturer:* Gloster Aircraft Co Ltd; *type:* fighter;
year: 1938; *engine:* Bristol Mercury VIII A 9-cylinder radial air-
cooled, 840 hp; *wingspan:* 32 ft 3 in (9.83 m); *length:* 27 ft 5 in
(8.36 m); *height:* 10 ft 2 in (3.10 m); *weight:* 4,850 lb (2,200 kg);
maximum speed: 257 mph (414 km/h) at 14,500 ft (4,420 m); *ceiling:* 33,490 ft (10,210 m); *range:* 444 miles (715 km); *armament:* 4
machine guns; *crew:* 1

FIAT CR 42
Nation: Italy; *manufacturer:* Fiat SA; *type:* fighter; *year:*
1939; *engine:* Fiat A.74 RC 38 14-cylinder radial air-
cooled, 840 hp; *wingspan:* 31 ft 10 in (9.70 m); *length:*
27 ft 3 in (8.30 m); *height:* 10 ft 10 in (3.30 m); *weight:*
5,060 lb (2,295 kg) (loaded); *maximum speed:*
273 mph (440 km/h) at 19,685 ft (6,000 m); *ceiling:*
34,450 ft (10,500 m); *range:* 490 miles (785 km);
armament: 2 machine guns; *crew:* 1

FIAT CR 42 CN
Nation: Italy; *manufacturer:* Fiat SA; *type:* fighter; *year:* 1941;
engine: Fiat A.47 RC 38 14-cylinder radial air-cooled, 840 hp;
wingspan: 31 ft 10 in (9.70 m); *length:* 27 ft 3 in (8.30 m); *height:*
10 ft 10 in (3.30 m); *weight:* 5,060 lb (2,295 kg) (loaded); *maximum
speed:* 273 mph (440 km/h) at 19,685 ft (6,000 m); *ceiling:*
34,450 ft (10,500 m); *range:* 490 miles (785 km); *armament:* 2
machine guns; *crew:* 1

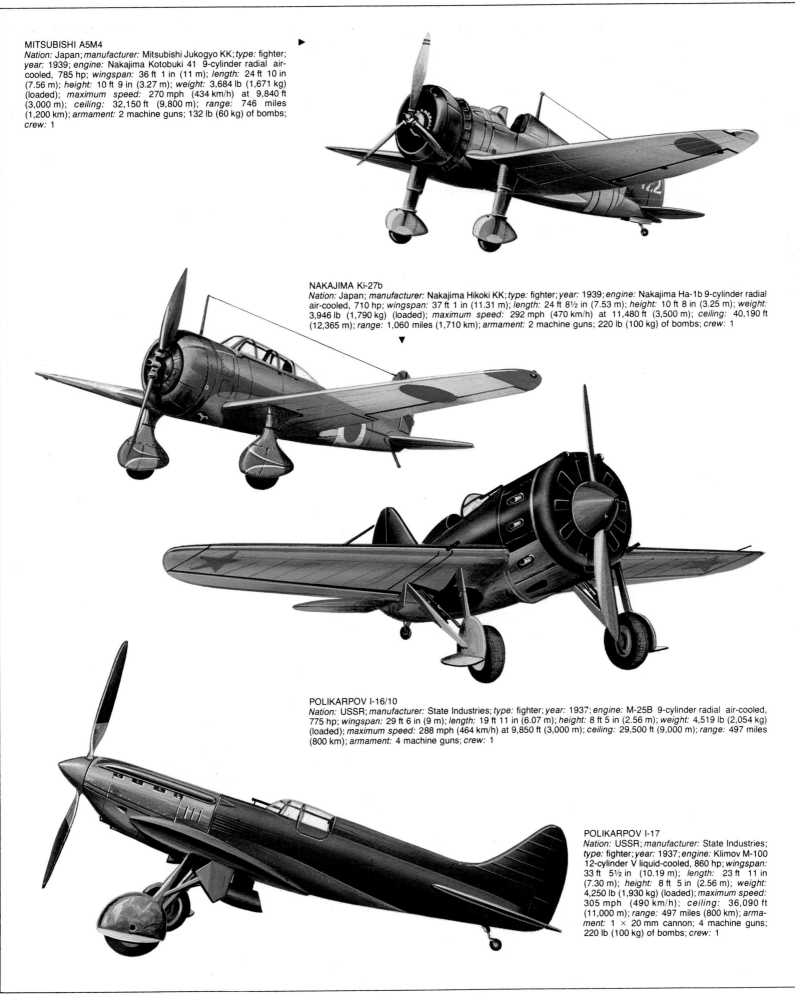

MITSUBISHI A5M4
Nation: Japan; *manufacturer:* Mitsubishi Jukogyo KK; *type:* fighter; *year:* 1939; *engine:* Nakajima Kotobuki 41 9-cylinder radial air-cooled, 785 hp; *wingspan:* 36 ft 1 in (11 m); *length:* 24 ft 10 in (7.56 m); *height:* 10 ft 9 in (3.27 m); *weight:* 3,684 lb (1,671 kg) (loaded); *maximum speed:* 270 mph (434 km/h) at 9,840 ft (3,000 m); *ceiling:* 32,150 ft (9,800 m); *range:* 746 miles (1,200 km); *armament:* 2 machine guns; 132 lb (60 kg) of bombs; *crew:* 1

NAKAJIMA Ki-27b
Nation: Japan; *manufacturer:* Nakajima Hikoki KK; *type:* fighter; *year:* 1939; *engine:* Nakajima Ha-1b 9-cylinder radial air-cooled, 710 hp; *wingspan:* 37 ft 1 in (11.31 m); *length:* 24 ft 8½ in (7.53 m); *height:* 10 ft 8 in (3.25 m); *weight:* 3,946 lb (1,790 kg) (loaded); *maximum speed:* 292 mph (470 km/h) at 11,480 ft (3,500 m); *ceiling:* 40,190 ft (12,365 m); *range:* 1,060 miles (1,710 km); *armament:* 2 machine guns; 220 lb (100 kg) of bombs; *crew:* 1

POLIKARPOV I-16/10
Nation: USSR; *manufacturer:* State Industries; *type:* fighter; *year:* 1937; *engine:* M-25B 9-cylinder radial air-cooled, 775 hp; *wingspan:* 29 ft 6 in (9 m); *length:* 19 ft 11 in (6.07 m); *height:* 8 ft 5 in (2.56 m); *weight:* 4,519 lb (2,054 kg) (loaded); *maximum speed:* 288 mph (464 km/h) at 9,850 ft (3,000 m); *ceiling:* 29,500 ft (9,000 m); *range:* 497 miles (800 km); *armament:* 4 machine guns; *crew:* 1

POLIKARPOV I-17
Nation: USSR; *manufacturer:* State Industries; *type:* fighter; *year:* 1937; *engine:* Klimov M-100 12-cylinder V liquid-cooled, 860 hp; *wingspan:* 33 ft 5½ in (10.19 m); *length:* 23 ft 11 in (7.30 m); *height:* 8 ft 5 in (2.56 m); *weight:* 4,250 lb (1,930 kg) (loaded); *maximum speed:* 305 mph (490 km/h); *ceiling:* 36,090 ft (11,000 m); *range:* 497 miles (800 km); *armament:* 1 × 20 mm cannon; 4 machine guns; 220 lb (100 kg) of bombs; *crew:* 1

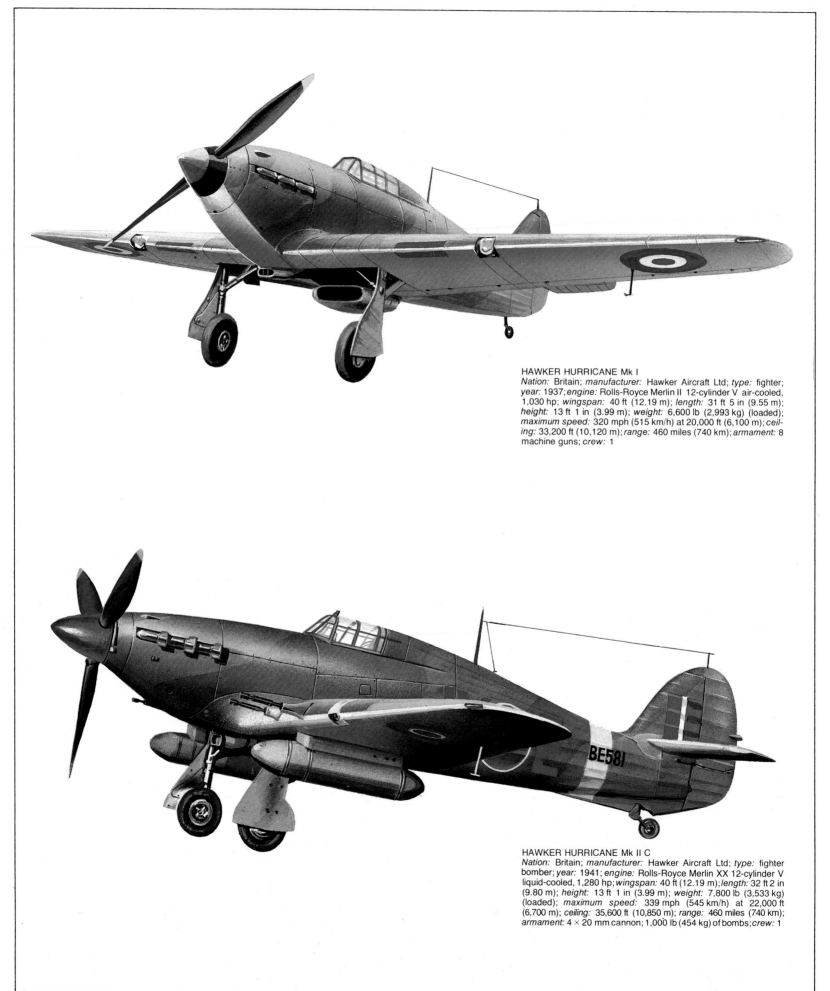

HAWKER HURRICANE Mk I
Nation: Britain; *manufacturer:* Hawker Aircraft Ltd; *type:* fighter; *year:* 1937; *engine:* Rolls-Royce Merlin II 12-cylinder V air-cooled, 1,030 hp; *wingspan:* 40 ft (12.19 m); *length:* 31 ft 5 in (9.55 m); *height:* 13 ft 1 in (3.99 m); *weight:* 6,600 lb (2,993 kg) (loaded); *maximum speed:* 320 mph (515 km/h) at 20,000 ft (6,100 m); *ceiling:* 33,200 ft (10,120 m); *range:* 460 miles (740 km); *armament:* 8 machine guns; *crew:* 1

HAWKER HURRICANE Mk II C
Nation: Britain; *manufacturer:* Hawker Aircraft Ltd; *type:* fighter bomber; *year:* 1941; *engine:* Rolls-Royce Merlin XX 12-cylinder V liquid-cooled, 1,280 hp; *wingspan:* 40 ft (12.19 m); *length:* 32 ft 2 in (9.80 m); *height:* 13 ft 1 in (3.99 m); *weight:* 7,800 lb (3,533 kg) (loaded); *maximum speed:* 339 mph (545 km/h) at 22,000 ft (6,700 m); *ceiling:* 35,600 ft (10,850 m); *range:* 460 miles (740 km); *armament:* 4 × 20 mm cannon; 1,000 lb (454 kg) of bombs; *crew:* 1

SUPERMARINE SPITFIRE Mk I
Nation: Britain; *manufacturer:* Supermarine Division of Vickers-Armstrong Ltd; *type:* fighter; *year:* 1938; *engine:* Rolls-Royce Merlin II 12-cylinder V liquid-cooled, 1,030 hp; *wingspan:* 36 ft 10 in (11.22 m); *length:* 29 ft 11 in (9.12 m); *height:* 11 ft 5 in (3.48 m); *weight:* 5,332 lb (2,415 kg) (loaded); *maximum speed:* 355 mph (571 km/h) at 19,000 ft (5,800 m); *ceiling:* 34,000 ft (10,360 m); *range:* 500 miles (805 km); *armament:* 8 machine guns; *crew:* 1

SUPERMARINE SPITFIRE Mk VB
Nation: Britain; *manufacturer:* Supermarine Division of Vickers-Armstrong Ltd; *type:* fighter; *year:* 1941; *engine:* Rolls-Royce Merlin 45 12-cylinder V liquid-cooled, 1,440 hp; *wingspan:* 36 ft 10 in (11.22 m); *length:* 29 ft 11 in (9.12 m); *height:* 11 ft 5 in (3.43 m); *weight:* 6,417 lb (2,911 kg) (loaded); *maximum speed:* 374 mph (602 km/h) at 13,000 ft (4,000 m); *ceiling:* 37,000 ft (11,280 m); *range:* 470 miles (750 km); *armament:* 2 × 20 mm cannon; 4 machine guns; *crew:* 1

SUPERMARINE SPITFIRE Mk IX
Nation: Britain; *manufacturer:* Supermarine Division of Vickers-Armstrong Ltd; *type:* fighter; *year:* 1942; *engine:* Rolls-Royce Merlin 61 12-cylinder V liquid-cooled, 1,515 hp; *wingspan:* 36 ft 10 in (11.22 m); *length:* 30 ft 6 in (9.30 m); *height:* 11 ft 5 in (3.48 m); *weight:* 7,500 lb (3,400 kg) (loaded); *maximum speed:* 408 mph (656 km/h) at 25,000 ft (7,620 m); *ceiling:* 44,000 ft (13,400 m); *range:* 434 miles (700 km); *armament:* 2 × 20 mm cannon; 4 machine guns; *crew:* 1

SUPERMARINE SPITFIRE Mk XIV
Nation: Britain; *manufacturer:* Supermarine Division of Vickers-Armstrong Ltd; *type:* fighter; *year:* 1944; *engine:* Rolls-Royce Griffon 65 12-cylinder V liquid-cooled, 2,050 hp; *wingspan:* 36 ft 10 in (11.22 m); *length:* 32 ft 8 in (9.95 m); *height:* 12 ft 8 in (3.86 m); *weight:* 8,500 lb (3,850 kg) (loaded); *maximum speed:* 448 mph (721 km/h) at 26,000 ft (7,900 m); *ceiling:* 44,500 ft (13,560 m); *range:* 460 miles (740 km); *armament:* 2 × 20 mm cannon; 4 machine guns; 1,000 lb (454 kg) of bombs; *crew:* 1

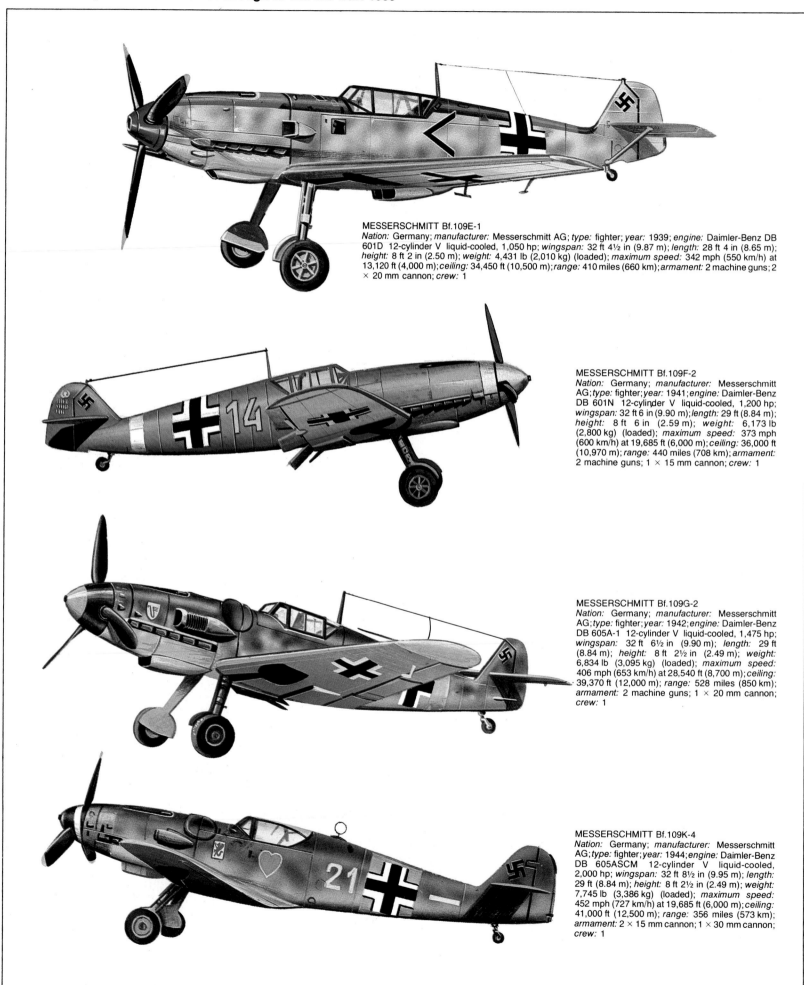

MESSERSCHMITT Bf.109E-1
Nation: Germany; *manufacturer:* Messerschmitt AG; *type:* fighter; *year:* 1939; *engine:* Daimler-Benz DB 601D 12-cylinder V liquid-cooled, 1,050 hp; *wingspan:* 32 ft 4½ in (9.87 m); *length:* 28 ft 4 in (8.65 m); *height:* 8 ft 2 in (2.50 m); *weight:* 4,431 lb (2,010 kg) (loaded); *maximum speed:* 342 mph (550 km/h) at 13,120 ft (4,000 m); *ceiling:* 34,450 ft (10,500 m); *range:* 410 miles (660 km); *armament:* 2 machine guns; 2 × 20 mm cannon; *crew:* 1

MESSERSCHMITT Bf.109F-2
Nation: Germany; *manufacturer:* Messerschmitt AG; *type:* fighter; *year:* 1941; *engine:* Daimler-Benz DB 601N 12-cylinder V liquid-cooled, 1,200 hp; *wingspan:* 32 ft 6 in (9.90 m); *length:* 29 ft (8.84 m); *height:* 8 ft 6 in (2.59 m); *weight:* 6,173 lb (2,800 kg) (loaded); *maximum speed:* 373 mph (600 km/h) at 19,685 ft (6,000 m); *ceiling:* 36,000 ft (10,970 m); *range:* 440 miles (708 km); *armament:* 2 machine guns; 1 × 15 mm cannon; *crew:* 1

MESSERSCHMITT Bf.109G-2
Nation: Germany; *manufacturer:* Messerschmitt AG; *type:* fighter; *year:* 1942; *engine:* Daimler-Benz DB 605A-1 12-cylinder V liquid-cooled, 1,475 hp; *wingspan:* 32 ft 6½ in (9.90 m); *length:* 29 ft (8.84 m); *height:* 8 ft 2½ in (2.49 m); *weight:* 6,834 lb (3,095 kg) (loaded); *maximum speed:* 406 mph (653 km/h) at 28,540 ft (8,700 m); *ceiling:* 39,370 ft (12,000 m); *range:* 528 miles (850 km); *armament:* 2 machine guns; 1 × 20 mm cannon; *crew:* 1

MESSERSCHMITT Bf.109K-4
Nation: Germany; *manufacturer:* Messerschmitt AG; *type:* fighter; *year:* 1944; *engine:* Daimler-Benz DB 605ASCM 12-cylinder V liquid-cooled, 2,000 hp; *wingspan:* 32 ft 8½ in (9.95 m); *length:* 29 ft (8.84 m); *height:* 8 ft 2½ in (2.49 m); *weight:* 7,745 lb (3,386 kg) (loaded); *maximum speed:* 452 mph (727 km/h) at 19,685 ft (6,000 m); *ceiling:* 41,000 ft (12,500 m); *range:* 356 miles (573 km); *armament:* 2 × 15 mm cannon; 1 × 30 mm cannon; *crew:* 1

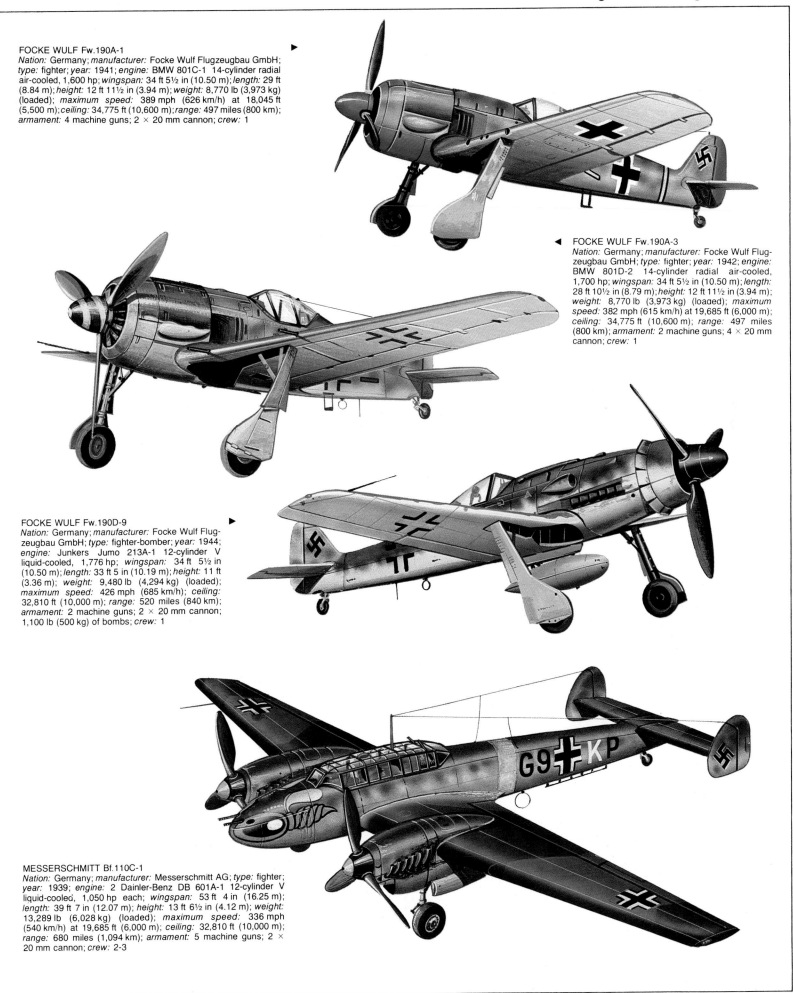

FOCKE WULF Fw.190A-1
Nation: Germany; *manufacturer:* Focke Wulf Flugzeugbau GmbH;
type: fighter; *year:* 1941; *engine:* BMW 801C-1 14-cylinder radial
air-cooled, 1,600 hp; *wingspan:* 34 ft 5½ in (10.50 m); *length:* 29 ft
(8.84 m); *height:* 12 ft 11½ in (3.94 m); *weight:* 8,770 lb (3,973 kg)
(loaded); *maximum speed:* 389 mph (626 km/h) at 18,045 ft
(5,500 m); *ceiling:* 34,775 ft (10,600 m); *range:* 497 miles (800 km);
armament: 4 machine guns; 2 × 20 mm cannon; *crew:* 1

FOCKE WULF Fw.190A-3
Nation: Germany; *manufacturer:* Focke Wulf Flugzeugbau GmbH; *type:* fighter; *year:* 1942; *engine:*
BMW 801D-2 14-cylinder radial air-cooled,
1,700 hp; *wingspan:* 34 ft 5½ in (10.50 m); *length:*
28 ft 10½ in (8.79 m); *height:* 12 ft 11½ in (3.94 m);
weight: 8,770 lb (3,973 kg) (loaded); *maximum
speed:* 382 mph (615 km/h) at 19,685 ft (6,000 m);
ceiling: 34,775 ft (10,600 m); *range:* 497 miles
(800 km); *armament:* 2 machine guns; 4 × 20 mm
cannon; *crew:* 1

FOCKE WULF Fw.190D-9
Nation: Germany; *manufacturer:* Focke Wulf Flugzeugbau GmbH; *type:* fighter-bomber; *year:* 1944;
engine: Junkers Jumo 213A-1 12-cylinder V
liquid-cooled, 1,776 hp; *wingspan:* 34 ft 5½ in
(10.50 m); *length:* 33 ft 5 in (10.19 m); *height:* 11 ft
(3.36 m); *weight:* 9,480 lb (4,294 kg) (loaded);
maximum speed: 426 mph (685 km/h); *ceiling:*
32,810 ft (10,000 m); *range:* 520 miles (840 km);
armament: 2 machine guns; 2 × 20 mm cannon;
1,100 lb (500 kg) of bombs; *crew:* 1

MESSERSCHMITT Bf.110C-1
Nation: Germany; *manufacturer:* Messerschmitt AG; *type:* fighter;
year: 1939; *engine:* 2 Dainler-Benz DB 601A-1 12-cylinder V
liquid-cooled, 1,050 hp each; *wingspan:* 53 ft 4 in (16.25 m);
length: 39 ft 7 in (12.07 m); *height:* 13 ft 6½ in (4.12 m); *weight:*
13,289 lb (6,028 kg) (loaded); *maximum speed:* 336 mph
(540 km/h) at 19,685 ft (6,000 m); *ceiling:* 32,810 ft (10,000 m);
range: 680 miles (1,094 km); *armament:* 5 machine guns; 2 ×
20 mm cannon; *crew:* 2-3

First and second generation Italian fighters of the Second World War: 1939–41

FIAT G.50
Nation: Italy; *manufacturer:* Fiat SA; *type:* fighter; *year:* 1939; *engine:* Fiat A.74 RC 38 14-cylinder radial air-cooled, 840 hp; *wingspan:* 36 ft (10.98 m); *length:* 25 ft 7 in (7.80 m); *height:* 9 ft 8½ in (2.95 m); *weight:* 5,280 lb (2,395 kg) (loaded); *maximum speed:* 294 mph (473 km/h) at 19,685 ft (6,000 m); *ceiling:* 35,200 ft (10,700 m); *range:* 420 miles (675 km); *armament:* 2 machine guns; *crew:* 1

MACCHI MC.200
Nation: Italy; *manufacturer:* Aeronautica Macchi SpA; *type:* fighter; *year:* 1939; *engine:* Fiat A.74 RC 38 14-cylinder radial air-cooled, 870 hp; *wingspan:* 34 ft 8½ in (10.57 m); *length:* 26 ft 11 in (8.19 m); *height:* 11 ft 6 in (3.51 m); *weight:* 4,874 lb (2,208 kg) (loaded); *maximum speed:* 318 mph (512 km/h) at 16,400 ft (5,000 m); *ceiling:* 28,700 ft (8,750 m); *range:* 540 miles (870 km); *armament:* 2 machine guns; *crew:* 1

MACCHI MC.202
Nation: Italy; *manufacturer:* Aeronautica Macchi SpA; *type:* fighter; *year:* 1941; *engine:* Daimler-Benz 601A-1 12-cylinder V liquid-cooled, 1,175 hp; *wingspan:* 34 ft 8½ in (10.58 m); *length:* 29 ft 1 in (8.85 m); *height:* 9 ft 11½ in (3.02 m); *weight:* 6,480 lb (2,937 kg) (loaded); *maximum speed:* 372 mph (600 km/h) at 18,050 ft (5,500 m); *ceiling:* 37,700 ft (11,500 m); *range:* 475 miles (765 km); *armament:* 2 machine guns; *crew:* 1

CAPRONI-REGGIANE Re 2000
Nation: Italy; *manufacturer:* Officine Meccaniche 'Reggiane' SpA (Caproni); *type:* fighter; *year:* 1939; *engine:* Piaggio P.XI RC 40 14-cylinder radial air-cooled, 986 hp; *wingspan:* 36 ft 1 in (11.00 m); *length:* 26 ft 2½ in (7.99 m); *height:* 10 ft 6 in (3.20 m); *weight:* 6,290 lb (2,850 m) (loaded); *maximum speed:* 329 mph (530 km/h) at 16,400 ft (5,000 m); *ceiling:* 34,450 ft (10,500 m); *range:* 870 miles (1,400 km); *armament:* 2 machine guns; *crew:* 1

CAPRONI-REGGIANE Re 2001
Nation: Italy; *manufacturer:* Officine Meccaniche 'Reggiane' SpA (Caproni); *type:* interceptor fighter; *year:* 1941: *engine:* Daimler-Benz DB 601A-1 12-cylinder V, liquid-cooled, 1,175 hp; *wingspan:* 36 ft 1 in (11.00 m); *length:* 27 ft 5 in (8.36 m); *height:* 10 ft 4 in (3.15 m); *weight:* 6,700 lb (3,040 kg) (loaded); *maximum speed:* 349 mph (563 km/h) at 17,700 ft (5,400 m); *ceiling:* 36,000 ft (11,000 m); *range:* 684 miles (1,100 km); *armament:* 4 machine guns; *crew:* 1

DEWOITINE D.520
Nation: France; *manufacturer:* SNCAM; *type:* fighter; *year:* 1940; *engine:* Hispano-Suiza 12Y 12-cylinder V liquid-cooled, 910 hp; *wingspan:* 33 ft 5 in (10.18 m); *length:* 28 ft 9 in (8.76 m); *height:* 8 ft 5 in (2.56 m); *weight:* 6,144 lb (2,780 kg) (loaded); *maximum speed:* 329 mph (529 km/h) at 19,685 ft (6,000 m); *ceiling:* 36,090 ft (11,000 m); *range:* 620 miles (998 km); *armament:* 1 × 20 mm cannon; 4 machine guns; *crew:* 1

ARSENAL VG-33
Nation: France; *manufacturer:* Arsenal de l'Aéronautique; *type:* fighter; *year:* 1940; *engine:* Hispano-Suiza 12Y 12-cylinder V liquid-cooled, 860 hp; *wingspan:* 35 ft 5 in (10.80 m); *length:* 28 ft 4 in (8.64 m); *height:* 10 ft 10 in (3.30 m); *weight:* 6,393 lb (2,896 kg) (loaded); *maximum speed:* 347 mph (558 km/h) at 17,060 ft (5,200 m); *ceiling:* 36,090 ft (11,000 m); *range:* 745 miles (1,200 km); *armament:* 1 × 20 mm cannon; 4 machine guns; *crew:* 1

ROGOZARSKI IK-3
Nation: Yugoslavia; *manufacturer:* Rogozarski AD; *type:* fighter; *year:* 1940; *engine:* Avia-Hispano-Suiza 12 Ycrs 12-cylinder V, liquid-cooled, 920 hp; *wingspan:* 33 ft 9½ in (10.28 m); *length:* 27 ft 5 in (8.35 m); *height:* 10 ft 8 in (3.25 m); *weight:* 5,291 lb (2,400 kg) (loaded); *maximum speed:* 327 mph (526 km/h) at 17,715 ft (5,400 m); *ceiling:* 26,250 ft (8,000 m); *range:* 310 miles (500 km); *armament:* 1 × 20 mm cannon; 2 machine guns; *crew:* 1

British fighters of 1940

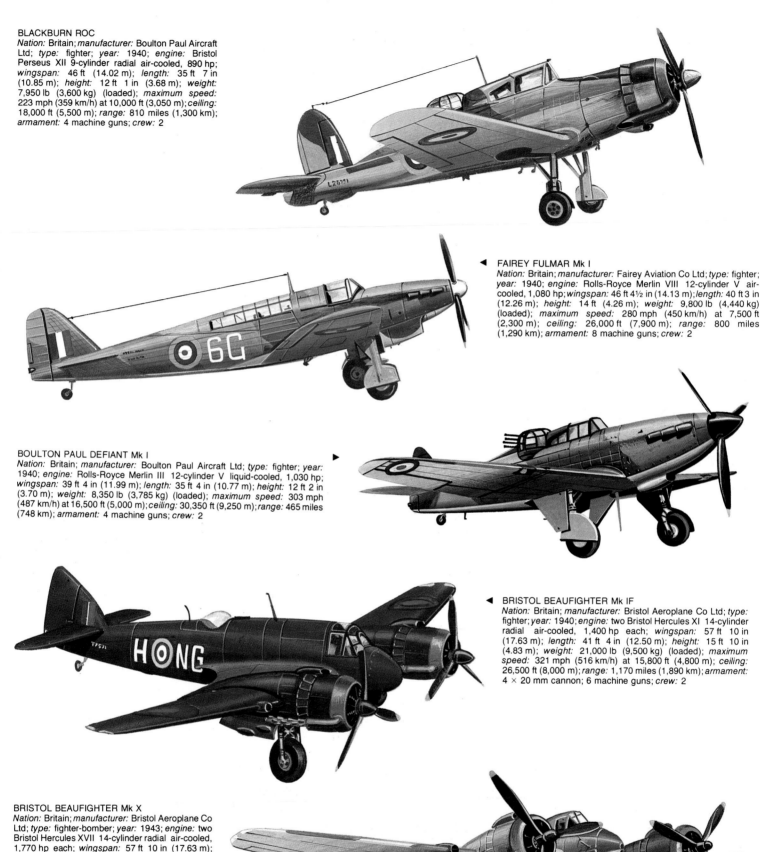

BLACKBURN ROC
Nation: Britain; *manufacturer:* Boulton Paul Aircraft Ltd; *type:* fighter; *year:* 1940; *engine:* Bristol Perseus XII 9-cylinder radial air-cooled, 890 hp; *wingspan:* 46 ft (14.02 m); *length:* 35 ft 7 in (10.85 m); *height:* 12 ft 1 in (3.68 m); *weight:* 7,950 lb (3,600 kg) (loaded); *maximum speed:* 223 mph (359 km/h) at 10,000 ft (3,050 m); *ceiling:* 18,000 ft (5,500 m); *range:* 810 miles (1,300 km); *armament:* 4 machine guns; *crew:* 2

FAIREY FULMAR Mk I
Nation: Britain; *manufacturer:* Fairey Aviation Co Ltd; *type:* fighter; *year:* 1940; *engine:* Rolls-Royce Merlin VIII 12-cylinder V air-cooled, 1,080 hp; *wingspan:* 46 ft 4½ in (14.13 m); *length:* 40 ft 3 in (12.26 m); *height:* 14 ft (4.26 m); *weight:* 9,800 lb (4,440 kg) (loaded); *maximum speed:* 280 mph (450 km/h) at 7,500 ft (2,300 m); *ceiling:* 26,000 ft (7,900 m); *range:* 800 miles (1,290 km); *armament:* 8 machine guns; *crew:* 2

BOULTON PAUL DEFIANT Mk I
Nation: Britain; *manufacturer:* Boulton Paul Aircraft Ltd; *type:* fighter; *year:* 1940; *engine:* Rolls-Royce Merlin III 12-cylinder V liquid-cooled, 1,030 hp; *wingspan:* 39 ft 4 in (11.99 m); *length:* 35 ft 4 in (10.77 m); *height:* 12 ft 2 in (3.70 m); *weight:* 8,350 lb (3,785 kg) (loaded); *maximum speed:* 303 mph (487 km/h) at 16,500 ft (5,000 m); *ceiling:* 30,350 ft (9,250 m); *range:* 465 miles (748 km); *armament:* 4 machine guns; *crew:* 2

BRISTOL BEAUFIGHTER Mk IF
Nation: Britain; *manufacturer:* Bristol Aeroplane Co Ltd; *type:* fighter; *year:* 1940; *engine:* two Bristol Hercules XI 14-cylinder radial air-cooled, 1,400 hp each; *wingspan:* 57 ft 10 in (17.63 m); *length:* 41 ft 4 in (12.50 m); *height:* 15 ft 10 in (4.83 m); *weight:* 21,000 lb (9,500 kg) (loaded); *maximum speed:* 321 mph (516 km/h) at 15,800 ft (4,800 m); *ceiling:* 26,500 ft (8,000 m); *range:* 1,170 miles (1,890 km); *armament:* 4 × 20 mm cannon; 6 machine guns; *crew:* 2

BRISTOL BEAUFIGHTER Mk X
Nation: Britain; *manufacturer:* Bristol Aeroplane Co Ltd; *type:* fighter-bomber; *year:* 1943; *engine:* two Bristol Hercules XVII 14-cylinder radial air-cooled, 1,770 hp each; *wingspan:* 57 ft 10 in (17.63 m); *length:* 42 ft 6 in (12.95 m); *height:* 15 ft 10 in (4.83 m); *weight:* 25,200 lb (11,430 kg) (loaded); *maximum speed:* 330 mph (531 km/h) at 1,300 ft (400 m); *ceiling:* 29,000 ft (8,800 m); *range:* 1,470 miles (2,365 km); *armament:* 4 × 20 mm cannon; 1 × 2,127 lb (964 kg) torpedo; 500 lb (226 kg) of bombs; *crew:* 2

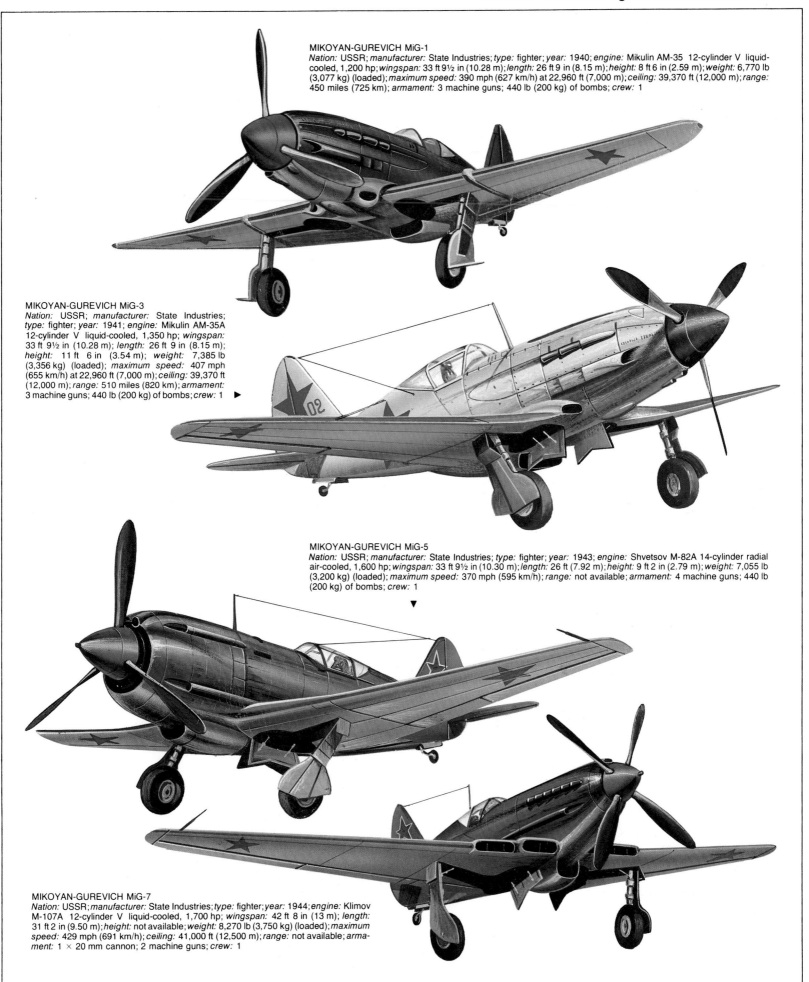

MIKOYAN-GUREVICH MiG-1
Nation: USSR; *manufacturer:* State Industries; *type:* fighter; *year:* 1940; *engine:* Mikulin AM-35 12-cylinder V liquid-cooled, 1,200 hp; *wingspan:* 33 ft 9½ in (10.28 m); *length:* 26 ft 9 in (8.15 m); *height:* 8 ft 6 in (2.59 m); *weight:* 6,770 lb (3,077 kg) (loaded); *maximum speed:* 390 mph (627 km/h) at 22,960 ft (7,000 m); *ceiling:* 39,370 ft (12,000 m); *range:* 450 miles (725 km); *armament:* 3 machine guns; 440 lb (200 kg) of bombs; *crew:* 1

MIKOYAN-GUREVICH MiG-3
Nation: USSR; *manufacturer:* State Industries; *type:* fighter; *year:* 1941; *engine:* Mikulin AM-35A 12-cylinder V liquid-cooled, 1,350 hp; *wingspan:* 33 ft 9½ in (10.28 m); *length:* 26 ft 9 in (8.15 m); *height:* 11 ft 6 in (3.54 m); *weight:* 7,385 lb (3,356 kg) (loaded); *maximum speed:* 407 mph (655 km/h) at 22,960 ft (7,000 m); *ceiling:* 39,370 ft (12,000 m); *range:* 510 miles (820 km); *armament:* 3 machine guns; 440 lb (200 kg) of bombs; *crew:* 1 ►

MIKOYAN-GUREVICH MiG-5
Nation: USSR; *manufacturer:* State Industries; *type:* fighter; *year:* 1943; *engine:* Shvetsov M-82A 14-cylinder radial air-cooled, 1,600 hp; *wingspan:* 33 ft 9½ in (10.30 m); *length:* 26 ft (7.92 m); *height:* 9 ft 2 in (2.79 m); *weight:* 7,055 lb (3,200 kg) (loaded); *maximum speed:* 370 mph (595 km/h); *range:* not available; *armament:* 4 machine guns; 440 lb (200 kg) of bombs; *crew:* 1
▼

MIKOYAN-GUREVICH MiG-7
Nation: USSR; *manufacturer:* State Industries; *type:* fighter; *year:* 1944; *engine:* Klimov M-107A 12-cylinder V liquid-cooled, 1,700 hp; *wingspan:* 42 ft 8 in (13 m); *length:* 31 ft 2 in (9.50 m); *height:* not available; *weight:* 8,270 lb (3,750 kg) (loaded); *maximum speed:* 429 mph (691 km/h); *ceiling:* 41,000 ft (12,500 m); *range:* not available; *armament:* 1 × 20 mm cannon; 2 machine guns; *crew:* 1

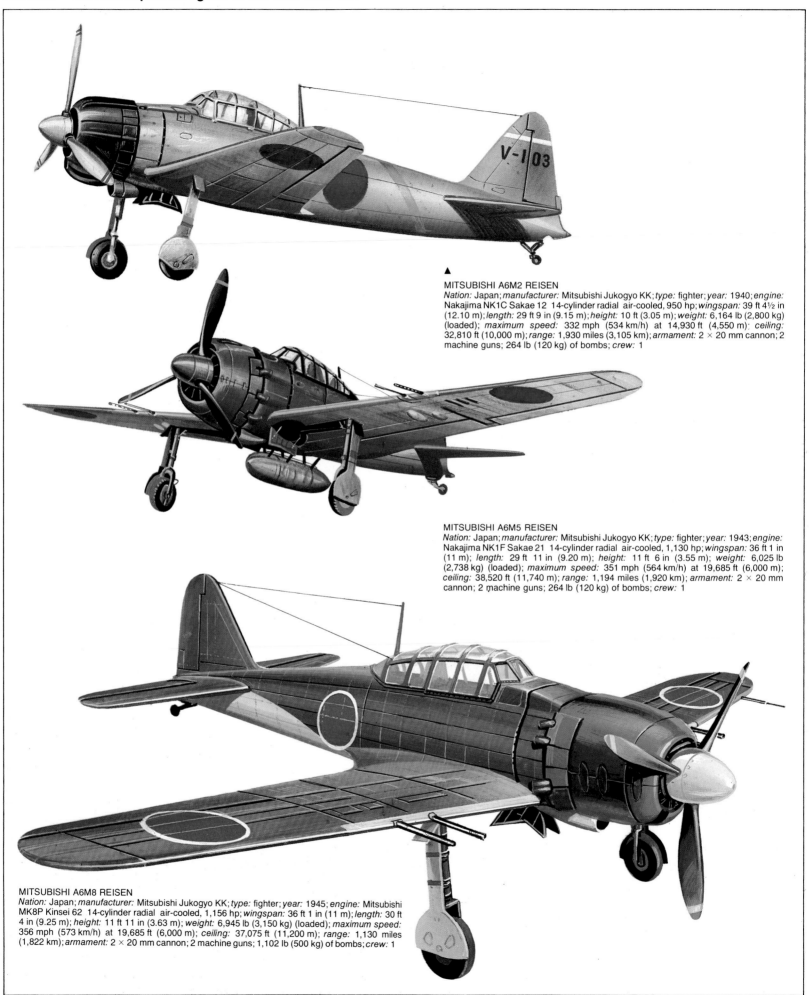

▲
MITSUBISHI A6M2 REISEN
Nation: Japan; *manufacturer:* Mitsubishi Jukogyo KK; *type:* fighter; *year:* 1940; *engine:* Nakajima NK1C Sakae 12 14-cylinder radial air-cooled, 950 hp; *wingspan:* 39 ft 4½ in (12.10 m); *length:* 29 ft 9 in (9.15 m); *height:* 10 ft (3.05 m); *weight:* 6,164 lb (2,800 kg) (loaded); *maximum speed:* 332 mph (534 km/h) at 14,930 ft (4,550 m); *ceiling:* 32,810 ft (10,000 m); *range:* 1,930 miles (3,105 km); *armament:* 2 × 20 mm cannon; 2 machine guns; 264 lb (120 kg) of bombs; *crew:* 1

MITSUBISHI A6M5 REISEN
Nation: Japan; *manufacturer:* Mitsubishi Jukogyo KK; *type:* fighter; *year:* 1943; *engine:* Nakajima NK1F Sakae 21 14-cylinder radial air-cooled, 1,130 hp; *wingspan:* 36 ft 1 in (11 m); *length:* 29 ft 11 in (9.20 m); *height:* 11 ft 6 in (3.55 m); *weight:* 6,025 lb (2,738 kg) (loaded); *maximum speed:* 351 mph (564 km/h) at 19,685 ft (6,000 m); *ceiling:* 38,520 ft (11,740 m); *range:* 1,194 miles (1,920 km); *armament:* 2 × 20 mm cannon; 2 machine guns; 264 lb (120 kg) of bombs; *crew:* 1

MITSUBISHI A6M8 REISEN
Nation: Japan; *manufacturer:* Mitsubishi Jukogyo KK; *type:* fighter; *year:* 1945; *engine:* Mitsubishi MK8P Kinsei 62 14-cylinder radial air-cooled, 1,156 hp; *wingspan:* 36 ft 1 in (11 m); *length:* 30 ft 4 in (9.25 m); *height:* 11 ft 11 in (3.63 m); *weight:* 6,945 lb (3,150 kg) (loaded); *maximum speed:* 356 mph (573 km/h) at 19,685 ft (6,000 m); *ceiling:* 37,075 ft (11,200 m); *range:* 1,130 miles (1,822 km); *armament:* 2 × 20 mm cannon; 2 machine guns; 1,102 lb (500 kg) of bombs; *crew:* 1

SEVERSKY P-35
Nation: USA; *manufacturer:* Republic Aviation Corp; *type:* fighter; *year:* 1937; *engine:* Pratt & Whitney R-1830-9 Twin Wasp 14-cylinder radial, air-cooled, 950 hp; *wingspan:* 36 ft (10.97 m); *length:* 25 ft 2 in (8.17 m); *height:* 9 ft 9 in (2.97 m); *weight:* 6,295 lb (2,855 kg) (loaded); *maximum speed:* 281 mph (453 km/h) at 10,000 ft (3,050 m); *ceiling:* 30,600 ft (9,330 m); *range:* 1,150 miles (1,850 km); *armament:* 2 machine guns; 300 lb (136 kg) of bombs; *crew:* 1

REPUBLIC P-43A LANCER
Nation: USA; *manufacturer:* Republic Aviation Corp; *type:* fighter-bomber; *year:* 1941; *engine:* Pratt & Whitney R-1830-49 Twin Wasp 14-cylinder radial air-cooled, 1,200 hp; *wingspan:* 36 ft (10.97 m); *length:* 28 ft 6 in (8.68 m); *height:* 14 ft (4.27 m); *weight:* 7,935 lb (3,600 kg) (loaded); *maximum speed:* 356 mph (570 km/h) at 25,000 ft (7,620 m); *ceiling:* 36,000 ft (11,000 m); *range:* 800 miles (1,290 km); *armament:* 4 machine guns; 200 lb (91 kg) of bombs; *crew:* 1

CURTISS P-36C
Nation: USA; *manufacturer:* Curtiss-Wright Corp; *type:* fighter; *year:* 1939; *engine:* Pratt & Whitney R-1830-17 Twin Wasp 14-cylinder radial air-cooled, 1,200 hp; *wingspan:* 37 ft 4 in (11.38 m); *length:* 28 ft 6 in (8.68 m); *height:* 12 ft 2 in (3.70 m); *weight:* 6,150 lb (2,790 kg) (loaded); *maximum speed:* 311 mph (500 km/h) at 10,000 ft (3,050 m); *ceiling:* 33,700 ft (10,300 m); *range:* 825 miles (1,320 km); *armament:* 2 machine guns; *crew:* 1

BELL P-39D AIRACOBRA
Nation: USA; *manufacturer:* Bell Aircraft Corp; *type:* fighter; *year:* 1941; *engine:* Allison V-1710-35 12-cylinder V liquid-cooled, 1,150 hp; *wingspan:* 34 ft (10.36 m); *length:* 30 ft 2 in (9.19 m); *height:* 11 ft 10 in (3.60 m); *weight:* 7,845 lb (3,520 kg) (loaded); *maximum speed:* 335 mph (536 km/h) at 13,800 ft (4,200 m); *ceiling:* 29,000 ft (8,900 m); *range:* 600 miles (960 km); *armament:* 1 × 37 mm cannon; 4 machine guns; 500 lb (226 kg) of bombs; *crew:* 1

BELL P-39Q AIRACOBRA
Nation: USA; *manufacturer:* Bell Aircraft Corp; *type:* fighter; *year:* 1943; *engine:* Allison V-1710-85 12-cylinder V liquid-cooled, 1,200 hp; *wingspan:* 34 ft (10.36 m); *length:* 30 ft 2 in (9.19 m); *height:* 12 ft 5 in (3.79 m); *weight:* 8,300 lb (3,765 kg) (loaded); *maximum speed:* 385 mph (620 km/h) at 11,000 ft (3,350 m); *ceiling:* 35,000 ft (10,670 m); *range:* 650 miles (1,046 km); *armament:* 1 × 37 mm cannon; 4 machine guns; 500 lb (226 kg) of bombs; *crew:* 1

The P-40 – the most important US fighter of America's first two years in the war: 1941–43

CURTISS P-40B WARHAWK
Nation: USA; *manufacturer:* Curtiss-Wright Corp;
type: fighter; *year:* 1941; *engine:* Allison V-1710-33
12-cylinder V liquid-cooled, 1,040 hp; *wingspan:*
37 ft 4 in (11.38 m); *length:* 31 ft 9 in (9.68 m);
height: 10 ft 7 in (3.23 m); *weight:* 7,600 lb
(3,450 kg) (loaded); *maximum speed:* 352 mph
(566 km/h) at 15,000 ft (4,572 m); *ceiling:* 32,400 ft
(9,875 m); *range:* 940 miles (1,500 km); *armament:*
4 machine guns; *crew:* 1

CURTISS P-40E WARHAWK
Nation: USA; *manufacturer:* Curtiss-Wright Corp;
type: fighter; *year:* 1942; *engine:* Allison V-1710-39
12-cylinder V liquid-cooled, 1,150 hp; *wingspan:*
37 ft 4 in (11.38 m); *length:* 31 ft 2 in (9.50 m);
height: 10 ft 7 in (3.23 m); *weight:* 9,200 lb
(3,900 kg) (loaded); *maximum speed:* 354 mph
(570 km/h) at 15,000 ft (4,572 m); *ceiling:* 29,000 ft
(8,840 m); *range:* 850 miles (1,360 km); *armament:*
6 machine guns; 700 lb (317 kg) of bombs; *crew:* 1

CURTISS P-40F WARHAWK
Nation: USA; *manufacturer:* Curtiss-Wright Corp;
type: fighter; *year:* 1942; *engine:* Packard
V-1650-1 12-cylinder V liquid-cooled, 1,300 hp;
wingspan: 37 ft 4 in (11.38 m); *length:* 33 ft 4 in
(10.16 m); *height:* 10 ft 4 in (3.23 m); *weight:*
9,350 lb (4,241 kg) (loaded); *maximum speed:*
364 mph (585 km/h) at 20,000 ft (6,100 m); *ceiling:*
34,400 ft (10,485 m); *range:* 375 miles (603 km);
armament: 6 machine guns; 500 lb (227 kg) of
bombs; *crew:* 1

CURTISS P-40N WARHAWK
Nation: USA; *manufacturer:* Curtiss-Wright Corp;
type: fighter; *year:* 1943; *engine:* Allison V-1710-81
12-cylinder V, liquid-cooled, 1,360 hp; *wingspan:*
37 ft 4 in (11.38 m); *length:* 33 ft 4 in (10.16 m);
height: 10 ft 4 in (3.23 m); *weight:* 8,850 lb
(4,014 kg) (loaded); *maximum speed:* 378 mph
(608 km/h) at 10,500 ft (3,200 m); *ceiling:* 38,000 ft
(11,580 m); *range:* 240 miles (386 km); *armament:*
6 machine guns; 500 lb (227 kg) of bombs; *crew:* 1

SUPERMARINE SEAFIRE Mk IIC
Nation: Britain; manufacturer: Supermarine Division of Vickers-Armstrong Ltd; type: fighter; year: 1942; engine: Rolls-Royce Merlin 45 12-cylinder V liquid-cooled, 1,340 hp; wingspan: 36 ft 8 in (11.17 m); length: 30 ft (9.14 m); height: 11 ft 2 in (3.41 m); weight: 7,000 lb (3,170 kg) (loaded); maximum speed: 333 mph (536 km/h) at 5,000 ft (1,500 m); ceiling: 32,000 ft (9,750 m); range: 755 miles (1,215 km); armament: 2 × 20 mm cannon; 4 machine guns; crew: 1

SUPERMARINE SEAFIRE Mk XV
Nation: Britain; manufacturer: Supermarine Division of Vickers-Armstrong Ltd; type: fighter; year: 1945; engine: Rolls-Royce Griffon VI 12-cylinder V liquid-cooled, 1,850 hp; wingspan: 36 ft 10 in (11.22 m); length: 32 ft 3 in (9.83 m); height: 10 ft 8 in (3.25 m); weight: 8,000 lb (3,628 kg) (loaded); maximum speed: 383 mph (616 km/h) at 13,500 ft (4,110 m); ceiling: 35,500 ft (10,810 m); range: 640 miles (1,029 km); armament: 2 × 20 mm cannon; 4 machine guns; crew: 1

FAIREY FIREFLY Mk I
Nation: Britain; manufacturer: Fairey Aviation Co Ltd; type: fighter; year: 1943; engine: Rolls-Royce Griffon IIB 12-cylinder V liquid-cooled, 1,730 hp; wingspan: 44 ft 6 in (13.56 m); length: 37 ft 7 in (11.46 m); height: 13 ft 7 in (4.14 m); weight: 14,020 lb (6,350 kg) (loaded); maximum speed: 316 mph (508 km/h) at 14,000 ft (4,250 m); ceiling: 28,000 ft (8,500 m); range: 1,300 miles (2,100 km); armament: 4 × 20 mm cannon; crew: 2

LAVOCHKIN LaGG-3
Nation: USSR; *manufacturer:* State Industries; *type:* fighter; *year:* 1941; *engine:* Klimov M-105PF 12-cylinder V liquid-cooled, 1,210 hp; *wingspan:* 32 ft 2 in (9.80 m); *length:* 29 ft 1 in (8.86 m); *height:* 8 ft 10 in (2.69 m); *weight:* 7,032 lb (3,190 kg) (loaded); *maximum speed:* 348 mph (560 km/h) at 16,400 ft (5,000 m); *ceiling:* 31,500 ft (9,690 m); *range:* 404 miles (650 km); *armament:* 1 × 20 mm cannon; 3 machine guns; 440 lb (200 kg) of bombs; *crew:* 1

LAVOCHKIN La-7
Nation: USSR; *manufacturer:* State Industries; *type:* fighter; *year:* 1944; *engine:* Shvetsov M-82FN 14-cylinder radial air-cooled, 1,850 hp; *wingspan:* 32 ft 2 in (9.80 m); *length:* 28 ft 2½ in (8.58 m); *height:* 9 ft 2 in (2.79 m); *weight:* 7,496 lb (3,400 kg) (loaded); *maximum speed:* 423 mph (680 km/h) at 21,000 ft (6,400 m); *ceiling:* 34,450 ft (10,500 m); *range:* 395 miles (635 km); *armament:* 3 × 20 mm cannon; 441 lb (200 kg) of bombs; *crew:* 1

LAVOCHKIN La-5FN
Nation: USSR; *manufacturer:* State Industries; *type:* fighter; *year:* 1943; *engine:* Shvetsov M-82FN 14-cylinder radial air-cooled, 1,640 hp; *wingspan:* 32 ft 2 in (9.80 m); *length:* 28 ft 5 in (8.65 m); *height:* 8 ft 4 in (2.56 m); *weight:* 7,406 lb (3,360 kg) (loaded); maximum *speed:* 402 mph (647 km/h) at 16,400 ft (5,000 m); *ceiling:* 32,800 ft (10,000 m); *range:* 475 miles (766 km); *armament:* 2 × 20 mm cannon; 662 lb (300 kg) of bombs; *crew:* 1

YAKOVLEV Yak-1
Nation: USSR; *manufacturer:* State Industries; *type:* fighter; *year:* 1942; *engine:* Klimov M-105PA 12-cylinder liquid-cooled, 1,100 hp; *wingspan:* 32 ft 10 in (10 m); *length:* 27 ft 9½ in (8.48 m); *height:* 8 ft 8 in (2.64 m); *weight:* 6,217 lb (2,820 kg) (loaded); *maximum speed:* 360 mph (580 km/h) at 16,400 ft (5,000 m); *ceiling:* 32,810 ft (10,000 m); *range:* 528 miles (850 km); *armament:* 1 × 20 mm cannon; 2 machine guns; *crew:* 1

YAKOVLEV Yak-9D
Nation: USSR; *manufacturer:* State Industries; *type:* fighter; *year:* 1943; *engine:* Klimov M-105PF 12-cylinder V liquid-cooled, 1,360 hp; *wingspan:* 32 ft 11½ in (10.03 m); *length:* 28 ft 1 in (8.55 m); *height:* 9 ft 10 in (3.05 m); *weight:* 6,867 lb (3,115 kg) (loaded); *maximum speed:* 374 mph (600 km/h) at 6,560 ft (2,000 m); *ceiling:* 32,800 ft (10,000 m); *range:* 808 miles (1,300 km); *armament:* 1 × 20 mm cannon; 1 machine gun; *crew:* 1

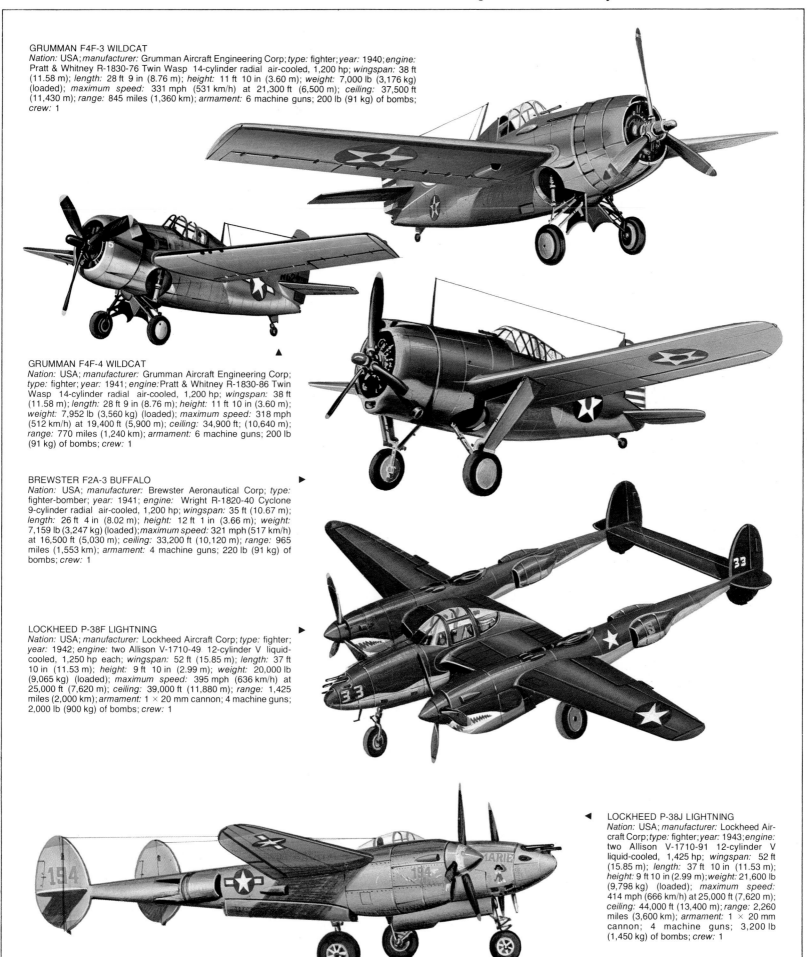

GRUMMAN F4F-3 WILDCAT
Nation: USA; manufacturer: Grumman Aircraft Engineering Corp; type: fighter; year: 1940; engine:
Pratt & Whitney R-1830-76 Twin Wasp 14-cylinder radial air-cooled, 1,200 hp; wingspan: 38 ft
(11.58 m); length: 28 ft 9 in (8.76 m); height: 11 ft 10 in (3.60 m); weight: 7,000 lb (3,176 kg)
(loaded); maximum speed: 331 mph (531 km/h) at 21,300 ft (6,500 m); ceiling: 37,500 ft
(11,430 m); range: 845 miles (1,360 km); armament: 6 machine guns; 200 lb (91 kg) of bombs;
crew: 1

GRUMMAN F4F-4 WILDCAT
Nation: USA; manufacturer: Grumman Aircraft Engineering Corp;
type: fighter; year: 1941; engine: Pratt & Whitney R-1830-86 Twin
Wasp 14-cylinder radial air-cooled, 1,200 hp; wingspan: 38 ft
(11.58 m); length: 28 ft 9 in (8.76 m); height: 11 ft 10 in (3.60 m);
weight: 7,952 lb (3,560 kg) (loaded); maximum speed: 318 mph
(512 km/h) at 19,400 ft (5,900 m); ceiling: 34,900 ft; (10,640 m);
range: 770 miles (1,240 km); armament: 6 machine guns; 200 lb
(91 kg) of bombs; crew: 1

BREWSTER F2A-3 BUFFALO
Nation: USA; manufacturer: Brewster Aeronautical Corp; type:
fighter-bomber; year: 1941; engine: Wright R-1820-40 Cyclone
9-cylinder radial air-cooled, 1,200 hp; wingspan: 35 ft (10.67 m);
length: 26 ft 4 in (8.02 m); height: 12 ft 1 in (3.66 m); weight:
7,159 lb (3,247 kg) (loaded); maximum speed: 321 mph (517 km/h)
at 16,500 ft (5,030 m); ceiling: 33,200 ft (10,120 m); range: 965
miles (1,553 km); armament: 4 machine guns; 220 lb (91 kg) of
bombs; crew: 1

LOCKHEED P-38F LIGHTNING
Nation: USA; manufacturer: Lockheed Aircraft Corp; type: fighter;
year: 1942; engine: two Allison V-1710-49 12-cylinder V liquid-
cooled, 1,250 hp each; wingspan: 52 ft (15.85 m); length: 37 ft
10 in (11.53 m); height: 9 ft 10 in (2.99 m); weight: 20,000 lb
(9,065 kg) (loaded); maximum speed: 395 mph (636 km/h) at
25,000 ft (7,620 m); ceiling: 39,000 ft (11,880 m); range: 1,425
miles (2,000 km); armament: 1 × 20 mm cannon; 4 machine guns;
2,000 lb (900 kg) of bombs; crew: 1

◀ LOCKHEED P-38J LIGHTNING
Nation: USA; manufacturer: Lockheed Aircraft Corp; type: fighter; year: 1943; engine:
two Allison V-1710-91 12-cylinder V
liquid-cooled, 1,425 hp; wingspan: 52 ft
(15.85 m); length: 37 ft 10 in (11.53 m);
height: 9 ft 10 in (2.99 m); weight: 21,600 lb
(9,798 kg) (loaded); maximum speed:
414 mph (666 km/h) at 25,000 ft (7,620 m);
ceiling: 44,000 ft (13,400 m); range: 2,260
miles (3,600 km); armament: 1 × 20 mm
cannon; 4 machine guns; 3,200 lb
(1,450 kg) of bombs; crew: 1

NAKAJIMA Ki-43-Ia HAYABUSA
Nation: Japan; *manufacturer:* Nakajima Hikoki KK; *type:* fighter; *year:* 1940; *engine:* Nakajima Ha-25 14-cylinder radial air-cooled, 980 hp; *wingspan:* 37 ft 6 in (11.43 m); *length:* 29 ft (8.85 m); *height:* 10 ft 9 in (3.29 m); *weight:* 5,695 lb (2,598 kg) (loaded); *maximum speed:* 308 mph (495 km/h) at 13,120 ft (4,000 m); *ceiling:* 38,500 ft (11,750 m); *range:* 745 miles (1,200 km); *armament:* 2 machine guns; 66 lb (30 kg) of bombs; *crew:* 1

NAKAJIMA Ki-43-IIb HAYABUSA
Nation: Japan; *manufacturer:* Nakajima Hikoki KK; *type:* fighter; *year:* 1942; *engine:* Nakajima Ha-115 14-cylinder radial air-cooled, 1,150 hp; *wingspan:* 35 ft 7 in (10.50 m); *length:* 29 ft 3 in (8.92 m); *height:* 10 ft.9 in (3.29 m); *weight:* 6,450 lb (2,932 kg) (loaded); *maximum speed:* 329 mph (530 km/h) at 13,125 ft (4,000 m); *ceiling:* 36,750 ft (11,200 m) *range:* 1,095 miles (1,760 km); *armament:* 2 machine guns; 1,102 lb (500 kg) of bombs; *crew:* 1

KAWASAKI Ki-45 KAIa TORYU
Nation: Japan; *manufacturer:* Kawasaki Kokuki Kogyo KK; *type:* fighter; *year:* 1942; *engine:* two Nakajima Ha-25 14-cylinder radial air-cooled, 1,050 hp each; *wingspan:* 49 ft 3 in (15.02 m); *length:* 34 ft 9 in (10.60 m); *height:* 12 ft 2 in (3.70 m); *weight:* 12,081 lb (5,491 kg) (loaded); *maximum speed:* 340 mph (547 km/h) at 22,965 ft (7,000 m); *ceiling:* 35,200 ft (10,730 m); *range:* 1,404 miles (2,260 km); *armament:* 1 × 20 mm cannon; 3 machine guns; 1,100 lb (500 kg) of bombs; *crew:* 2

NAKAJIMA A6M2-N
Nation: Japan; *manufacturer:* Nakajima Hikoki KK; *type:* fighter; *year:* 1942; *engine:* Nakajima NK1C Sakae 12 14-cylinder radial air-cooled, 950 hp; *wingspan:* 39 ft 4½ in (12 m); *length:* 33 ft 2 in (10.10 m); *height:* 14 ft 1 in (4.30 m); *weight:* 6,349 lb (2,895 kg); *maximum speed:* 270 mph (434 km/h) at 16,400 ft (5,000 m); *ceiling:* 32,810 ft (10,000 m); *range:* 1,107 miles (1,780 km); *armament:* 2 × 20 mm cannon; 2 machine guns; 264 lb (120 kg) of bombs; *crew:* 1

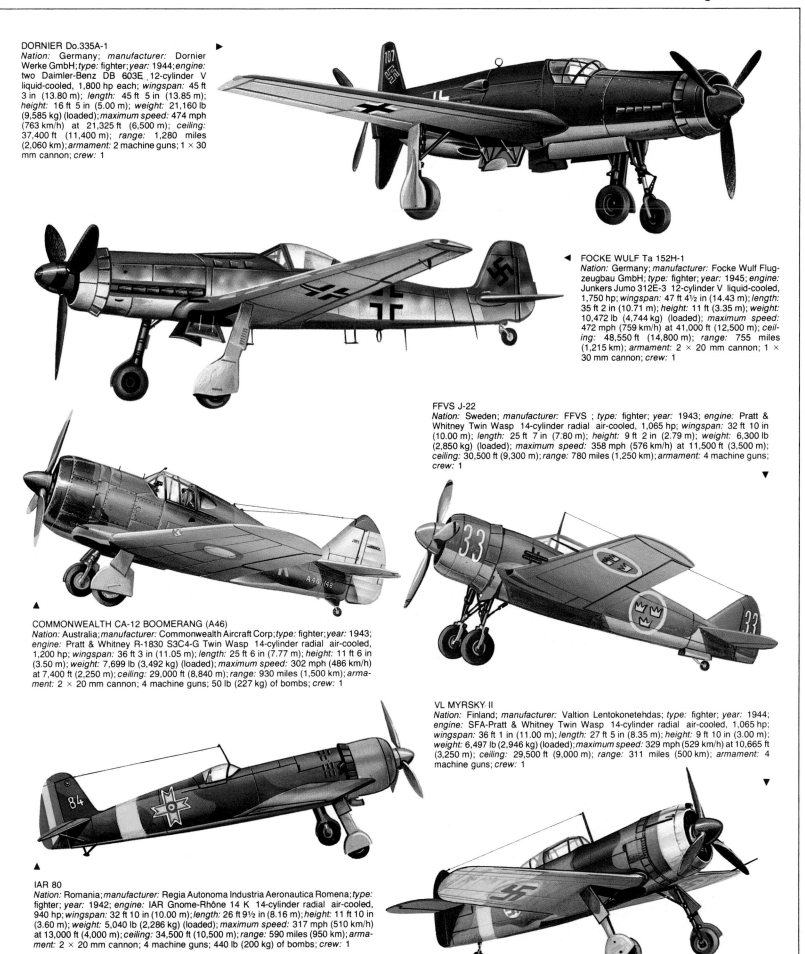

DORNIER Do.335A-1
Nation: Germany; *manufacturer:* Dornier Werke GmbH; *type:* fighter; *year:* 1944; *engine:* two Daimler-Benz DB 603E 12-cylinder V liquid-cooled, 1,800 hp each; *wingspan:* 45 ft 3 in (13.80 m); *length:* 45 ft 5 in (13.85 m); *height:* 16 ft 5 in (5.00 m); *weight:* 21,160 lb (9,585 kg) (loaded); *maximum speed:* 474 mph (763 km/h) at 21,325 ft (6,500 m); *ceiling:* 37,400 ft (11,400 m); *range:* 1,280 miles (2,060 km); *armament:* 2 machine guns; 1 × 30 mm cannon; *crew:* 1

FOCKE WULF Ta 152H-1
Nation: Germany; *manufacturer:* Focke Wulf Flugzeugbau GmbH; *type:* fighter; *year:* 1945; *engine:* Junkers Jumo 312E-3 12-cylinder V liquid-cooled, 1,750 hp; *wingspan:* 47 ft 4½ in (14.43 m); *length:* 35 ft 2 in (10.71 m); *height:* 11 ft (3.35 m); *weight:* 10,472 lb (4,744 kg) (loaded); *maximum speed:* 472 mph (759 km/h) at 41,000 ft (12,500 m); *ceiling:* 48,550 ft (14,800 m); *range:* 755 miles (1,215 km); *armament:* 2 × 20 mm cannon; 1 × 30 mm cannon; *crew:* 1

FFVS J-22
Nation: Sweden; *manufacturer:* FFVS ; *type:* fighter; *year:* 1943; *engine:* Pratt & Whitney Twin Wasp 14-cylinder radial air-cooled, 1,065 hp; *wingspan:* 32 ft 10 in (10.00 m); *length:* 25 ft 7 in (7.80 m); *height:* 9 ft 2 in (2.79 m); *weight:* 6,300 lb (2,850 kg) (loaded); *maximum speed:* 358 mph (576 km/h) at 11,500 ft (3,500 m); *ceiling:* 30,500 ft (9,300 m); *range:* 780 miles (1,250 km); *armament:* 4 machine guns; *crew:* 1

COMMONWEALTH CA-12 BOOMERANG (A46)
Nation: Australia; *manufacturer:* Commonwealth Aircraft Corp; *type:* fighter; *year:* 1943; *engine:* Pratt & Whitney R-1830 S3C4-G Twin Wasp 14-cylinder radial air-cooled, 1,200 hp; *wingspan:* 36 ft 3 in (11.05 m); *length:* 25 ft 6 in (7.77 m); *height:* 11 ft 6 in (3.50 m); *weight:* 7,699 lb (3,492 kg) (loaded); *maximum speed:* 302 mph (486 km/h) at 7,400 ft (2,250 m); *ceiling:* 29,000 ft (8,840 m); *range:* 930 miles (1,500 km); *armament:* 2 × 20 mm cannon; 4 machine guns; 50 lb (227 kg) of bombs; *crew:* 1

VL MYRSKY II
Nation: Finland; *manufacturer:* Valtion Lentokonetehdas; *type:* fighter; *year:* 1944; *engine:* SFA-Pratt & Whitney Twin Wasp 14-cylinder radial air-cooled, 1,065 hp; *wingspan:* 36 ft 1 in (11.00 m); *length:* 27 ft 5 in (8.35 m); *height:* 9 ft 10 in (3.00 m); *weight:* 6,497 lb (2,946 kg) (loaded); *maximum speed:* 329 mph (529 km/h) at 10,665 ft (3,250 m); *ceiling:* 29,500 ft (9,000 m); *range:* 311 miles (500 km); *armament:* 4 machine guns; *crew:* 1

IAR 80
Nation: Romania; *manufacturer:* Regia Autonoma Industria Aeronautica Romena; *type:* fighter; *year:* 1942; *engine:* IAR Gnome-Rhône 14 K 14-cylinder radial air-cooled, 940 hp; *wingspan:* 32 ft 10 in (10.00 m); *length:* 26 ft 9½ in (8.16 m); *height:* 11 ft 10 in (3.60 m); *weight:* 5,040 lb (2,286 kg) (loaded); *maximum speed:* 317 mph (510 km/h) at 13,000 ft (4,000 m); *ceiling:* 34,500 ft (10,500 m); *range:* 590 miles (950 km); *armament:* 2 × 20 mm cannon; 4 machine guns; 440 lb (200 kg) of bombs; *crew:* 1

MACCHI MC. 205
Nation: Italy; *manufacturer:* Aeronautica Macchi
SpA; *type:* fighter; *year:* 1943; *engine:* Daimler
Benz DB 605 A 12-cylinder V liquid-cooled,
1,475 hp; *wingspan:* 34 ft 8½ in (10.59 m); *length:*
29 ft 1 in (8.85 m); *height:* 10 ft (3.05 m); *weight:*
7,120 lb (3,224 kg) (loaded); *maximum speed:*
403 mph (650 km/h) at 24,300 ft (7,400 m); *ceiling:*
37,200 ft (11,350 m); *range:* 646 miles (1,040 km);
armament: 2 machine guns; 2 × 20 mm cannon;
crew: 1

FIAT G.55
Nation: Italy; *manufacturer:* Fiat SA; *type:* fighter;
year: 1943; *engine:* Daimler Benz DB 605 A 12-
cylinder V liquid-cooled, 1,475 hp; *wingspan:* 38 ft
10½ in (11.85 m); *length:* 30 ft 9 in (9.37 m); *height:*
12 ft 4 in (3.77 m); *weight:* 8,200 lb (3,720 kg)
(loaded); *maximum speed:* 385 mph (620 km/h) at
24,300 ft (7,400 m); *ceiling:* 41,700 ft (12,700 m);
range: 1,025 miles (1,650 km); *armament:* 2
machine guns; 3 × 20 mm cannon; *crew:* 1

◄ CAPRONI-REGGIANE Re 2005
Nation: Italy; *manufacturer:* Officine Meccaniche 'Reggiane' SpA (Caproni); *type:*
fighter; *year:* 1943; *engine:* Daimler Benz
DB 605 A 12-cylinder V liquid-cooled,
1,475 hp; *wingspan:* 36 ft 1 in (11.00 m);
length: 28 ft 8 in (8.73 m); *height:* 10 ft 4 in
(3.15 m); *weight:* 7,970 lb (3,610 kg)
(loaded); *maximum speed:* 421 mph
(678 km/h) at 22,800 ft (6,949 m); *ceiling:*
39,400 ft (12,000 m); *range:* 780 miles
(1,250 km); *armament:* 2 machine guns; 3
× 20 mm cannon; *crew:* 1

AMBROSINI SAI207
Nation: Italy; *manufacturer:* Società Aeronautica Italiana Ing. A. Ambrosini & C.; *type:*
fighter; *year:* 1943; *engine:* Isotta-Fraschini Delta RC 40 12-cylinder V air-cooled,
750 hp; *wingspan:* 29 ft 6 in (9.00 m); *length:* 26 ft 4 in (8.02 m); *height:* 9 ft 5 in
(2.88 m); *weight:* 5,330 lb (2,415 kg) (loaded); *maximum speed:* 388 mph (625 km/h);
ceiling: 39,400 ft (12,000 m); *range:* 528 miles (850 km); *armament:* 2 machine guns;
crew: 1

◄ MERIDIONALI Ro 57
Nation: Italy; *manufacturer:* SA Industrie Meccaniche & Aeronautiche Meridionali
(IMAM); *type:* fighter; *year:* 1943; *engine:* two Fiat A.74 RC 38 14-cylinder radial
air-cooled, 840 hp each; *wingspan:* 41 ft (12.50 m); *length:* 28 ft 11 in (8.80 m); *height:*
9 ft 6 in (2.90 m); *weight:* 8,950 lb (4,055 kg) (loaded); *maximum speed:* 320 mph
(516 km/h) at 17,200 ft (5,250 m); *ceiling:* 30,500 (9,300 m); *range:* 746 miles
(1,200 km); *armament:* 2 machine guns; *crew:* 1

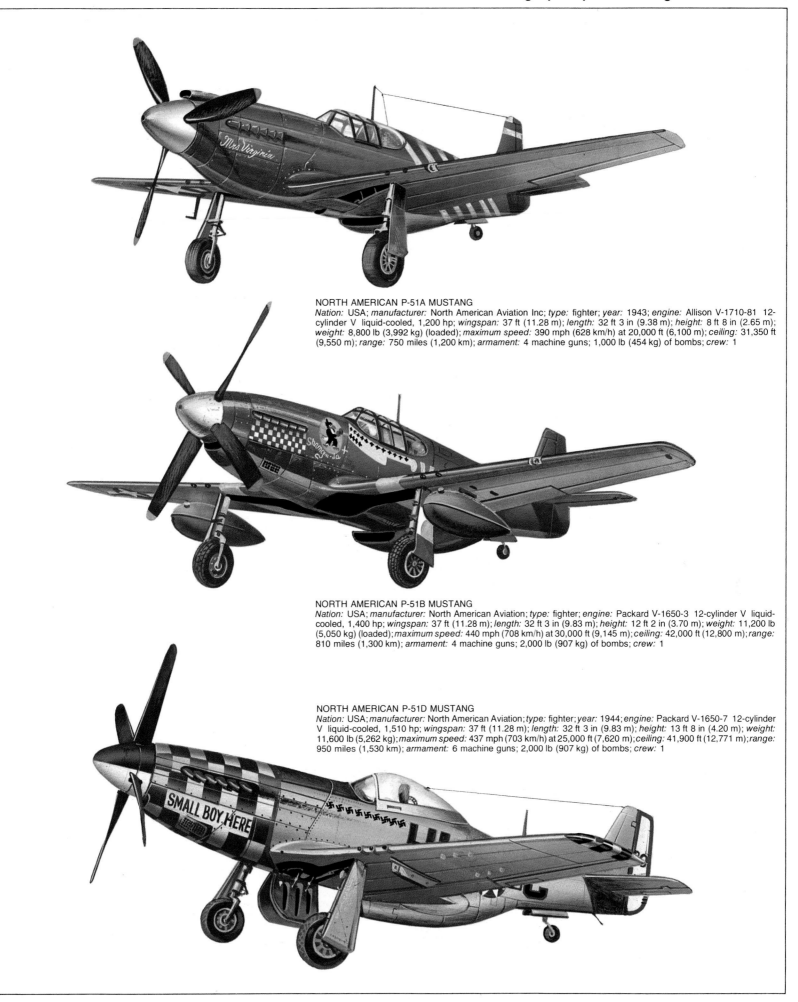

NORTH AMERICAN P-51A MUSTANG
Nation: USA; *manufacturer:* North American Aviation Inc; *type:* fighter; *year:* 1943; *engine:* Allison V-1710-81 12-cylinder V liquid-cooled, 1,200 hp; *wingspan:* 37 ft (11.28 m); *length:* 32 ft 3 in (9.38 m); *height:* 8 ft 8 in (2.65 m); *weight:* 8,800 lb (3,992 kg) (loaded); *maximum speed:* 390 mph (628 km/h) at 20,000 ft (6,100 m); *ceiling:* 31,350 ft (9,550 m); *range:* 750 miles (1,200 km); *armament:* 4 machine guns; 1,000 lb (454 kg) of bombs; *crew:* 1

NORTH AMERICAN P-51B MUSTANG
Nation: USA; *manufacturer:* North American Aviation; *type:* fighter; *engine:* Packard V-1650-3 12-cylinder V liquid-cooled, 1,400 hp; *wingspan:* 37 ft (11.28 m); *length:* 32 ft 3 in (9.83 m); *height:* 12 ft 2 in (3.70 m); *weight:* 11,200 lb (5,050 kg) (loaded); *maximum speed:* 440 mph (708 km/h) at 30,000 ft (9,145 m); *ceiling:* 42,000 ft (12,800 m); *range:* 810 miles (1,300 km); *armament:* 4 machine guns; 2,000 lb (907 kg) of bombs; *crew:* 1

NORTH AMERICAN P-51D MUSTANG
Nation: USA; *manufacturer:* North American Aviation; *type:* fighter; *year:* 1944; *engine:* Packard V-1650-7 12-cylinder V liquid-cooled, 1,510 hp; *wingspan:* 37 ft (11.28 m); *length:* 32 ft 3 in (9.83 m); *height:* 13 ft 8 in (4.20 m); *weight:* 11,600 lb (5,262 kg); *maximum speed:* 437 mph (703 km/h) at 25,000 ft (7,620 m); *ceiling:* 41,900 ft (12,771 m); *range:* 950 miles (1,530 km); *armament:* 6 machine guns; 2,000 lb (907 kg) of bombs; *crew:* 1

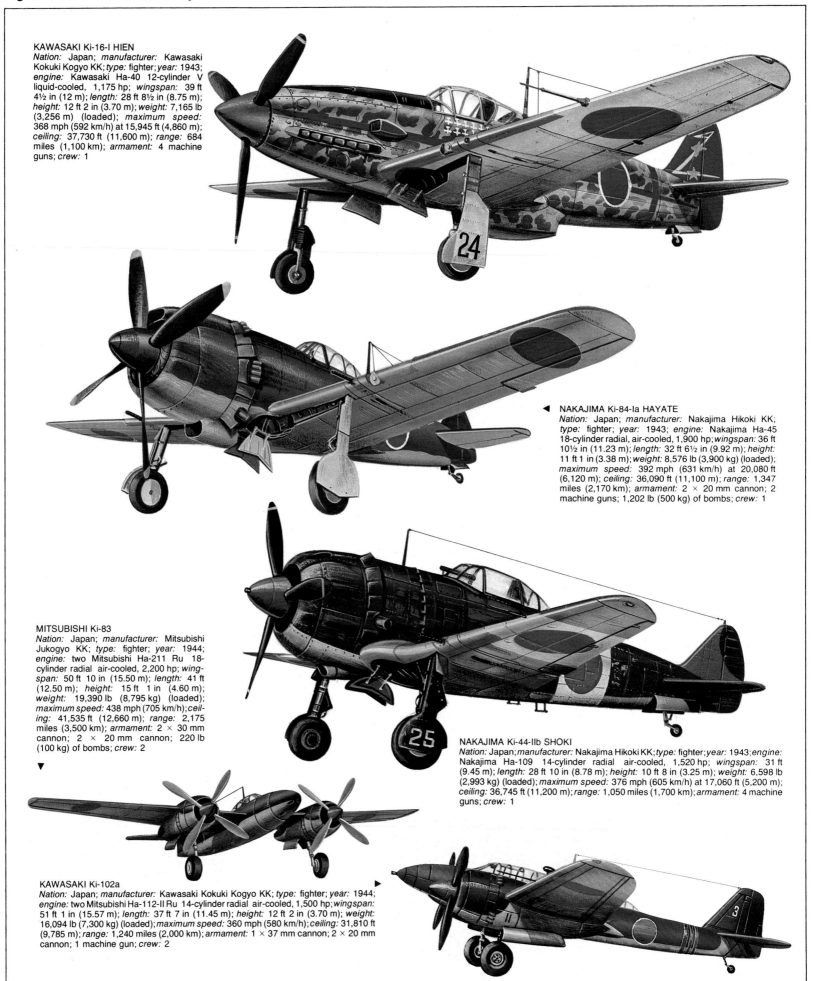

KAWASAKI Ki-16-I HIEN
Nation: Japan; *manufacturer:* Kawasaki Kokuki Kogyo KK; *type:* fighter; *year:* 1943; *engine:* Kawasaki Ha-40 12-cylinder V liquid-cooled, 1,175 hp; *wingspan:* 39 ft 4½ in (12 m); *length:* 28 ft 8½ in (8.75 m); *height:* 12 ft 2 in (3.70 m); *weight:* 7,165 lb (3,256 m) (loaded); *maximum speed:* 368 mph (592 km/h) at 15,945 ft (4,860 m); *ceiling:* 37,730 ft (11,600 m); *range:* 684 miles (1,100 km); *armament:* 4 machine guns; *crew:* 1

◄ NAKAJIMA Ki-84-Ia HAYATE
Nation: Japan; *manufacturer:* Nakajima Hikoki KK; *type:* fighter; *year:* 1943; *engine:* Nakajima Ha-45 18-cylinder radial, air-cooled, 1,900 hp; *wingspan:* 36 ft 10½ in (11.23 m); *length:* 32 ft 6½ in (9.92 m); *height:* 11 ft 1 in (3.38 m); *weight:* 8,576 lb (3,900 kg) (loaded); *maximum speed:* 392 mph (631 km/h) at 20,080 ft (6,120 m); *ceiling:* 36,090 ft (11,100 m); *range:* 1,347 miles (2,170 km); *armament:* 2 × 20 mm cannon; 2 machine guns; 1,202 lb (500 kg) of bombs; *crew:* 1

MITSUBISHI Ki-83
Nation: Japan; *manufacturer:* Mitsubishi Jukogyo KK; *type:* fighter; *year:* 1944; *engine:* two Mitsubishi Ha-211 Ru 18-cylinder radial air-cooled, 2,200 hp; *wingspan:* 50 ft 10 in (15.50 m); *length:* 41 ft (12.50 m); *height:* 15 ft 1 in (4.60 m); *weight:* 19,390 lb (8,795 kg) (loaded); *maximum speed:* 438 mph (705 km/h); *ceiling:* 41,535 ft (12,660 m); *range:* 2,175 miles (3,500 km); *armament:* 2 × 30 mm cannon; 2 × 20 mm cannon; 220 lb (100 kg) of bombs; *crew:* 2

▼

NAKAJIMA Ki-44-IIb SHOKI
Nation: Japan; *manufacturer:* Nakajima Hikoki KK; *type:* fighter; *year:* 1943; *engine:* Nakajima Ha-109 14-cylinder radial air-cooled, 1,520 hp; *wingspan:* 31 ft (9.45 m); *length:* 28 ft 10 in (8.78 m); *height:* 10 ft 8 in (3.25 m); *weight:* 6,598 lb (2,993 kg) (loaded); *maximum speed:* 376 mph (605 km/h) at 17,060 ft (5,200 m); *ceiling:* 36,745 ft (11,200 m); *range:* 1,050 miles (1,700 km); *armament:* 4 machine guns; *crew:* 1

KAWASAKI Ki-102a
Nation: Japan; *manufacturer:* Kawasaki Kokuki Kogyo KK; *type:* fighter; *year:* 1944; *engine:* two Mitsubishi Ha-112-II Ru 14-cylinder radial air-cooled, 1,500 hp; *wingspan:* 51 ft 1 in (15.57 m); *length:* 37 ft 7 in (11.45 m); *height:* 12 ft 2 in (3.70 m); *weight:* 16,094 lb (7,300 kg) (loaded); *maximum speed:* 360 mph (580 km/h); *ceiling:* 31,810 ft (9,785 m); *range:* 1,240 miles (2,000 km); *armament:* 1 × 37 mm cannon; 2 × 20 mm cannon; 1 machine gun; *crew:* 2 ▶

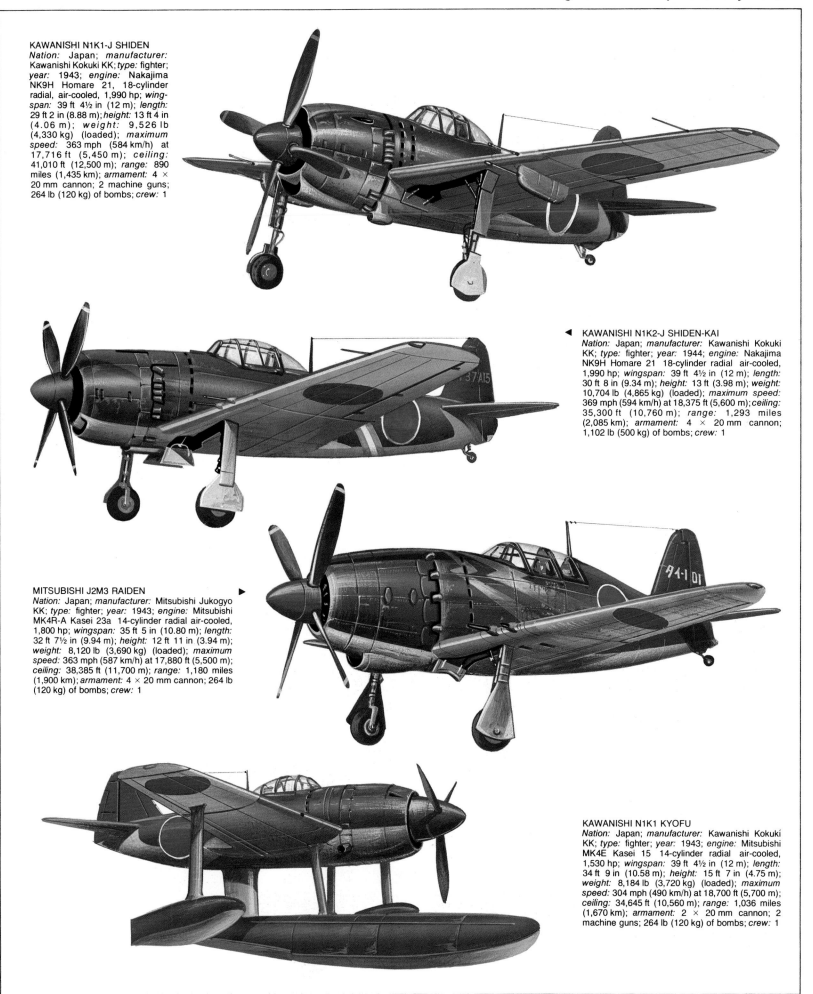

KAWANISHI N1K1-J SHIDEN
Nation: Japan; *manufacturer:* Kawanishi Kokuki KK; *type:* fighter; *year:* 1943; *engine:* Nakajima NK9H Homare 21, 18-cylinder radial, air-cooled, 1,990 hp; *wingspan:* 39 ft 4½ in (12 m); *length:* 29 ft 2 in (8.88 m); *height:* 13 ft 4 in (4.06 m); *weight:* 9,526 lb (4,330 kg) (loaded); *maximum speed:* 363 mph (584 km/h) at 17,716 ft (5,450 m); *ceiling:* 41,010 ft (12,500 m); *range:* 890 miles (1,435 km); *armament:* 4 × 20 mm cannon; 2 machine guns; 264 lb (120 kg) of bombs; *crew:* 1

◀ **KAWANISHI N1K2-J SHIDEN-KAI**
Nation: Japan; *manufacturer:* Kawanishi Kokuki KK; *type:* fighter; *year:* 1944; *engine:* Nakajima NK9H Homare 21 18-cylinder radial air-cooled, 1,990 hp; *wingspan:* 39 ft 4½ in (12 m); *length:* 30 ft 8 in (9.34 m); *height:* 13 ft (3.98 m); *weight:* 10,704 lb (4,865 kg) (loaded); *maximum speed:* 369 mph (594 km/h) at 18,375 ft (5,600 m); *ceiling:* 35,300 ft (10,760 m); *range:* 1,293 miles (2,085 km); *armament:* 4 × 20 mm cannon; 1,102 lb (500 kg) of bombs; *crew:* 1

MITSUBISHI J2M3 RAIDEN
Nation: Japan; *manufacturer:* Mitsubishi Jukogyo KK; *type:* fighter; *year:* 1943; *engine:* Mitsubishi MK4R-A Kasei 23a 14-cylinder radial air-cooled, 1,800 hp; *wingspan:* 35 ft 5 in (10.80 m); *length:* 32 ft 7½ in (9.94 m); *height:* 12 ft 11 in (3.94 m); *weight:* 8,120 lb (3,690 kg) (loaded); *maximum speed:* 363 mph (587 km/h) at 17,880 ft (5,500 m); *ceiling:* 38,385 ft (11,700 m); *range:* 1,180 miles (1,900 km); *armament:* 4 × 20 mm cannon; 264 lb (120 kg) of bombs; *crew:* 1

▶

KAWANISHI N1K1 KYOFU
Nation: Japan; *manufacturer:* Kawanishi Kokuki KK; *type:* fighter; *year:* 1943; *engine:* Mitsubishi MK4E Kasei 15 14-cylinder radial air-cooled, 1,530 hp; *wingspan:* 39 ft 4½ in (12 m); *length:* 34 ft 9 in (10.58 m); *height:* 15 ft 7 in (4.75 m); *weight:* 8,184 lb (3,720 kg) (loaded); *maximum speed:* 304 mph (490 km/h) at 18,700 ft (5,700 m); *ceiling:* 34,645 ft (10,560 m); *range:* 1,036 miles (1,670 km); *armament:* 2 × 20 mm cannon; 2 machine guns; 264 lb (120 kg) of bombs; *crew:* 1

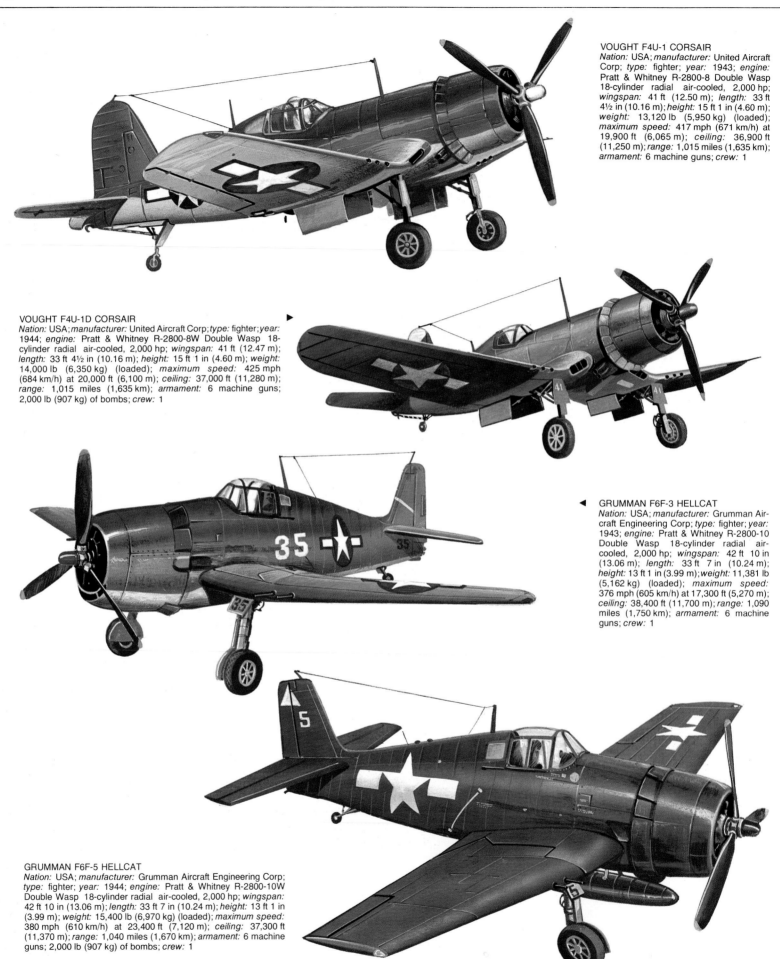

VOUGHT F4U-1 CORSAIR
Nation: USA; *manufacturer:* United Aircraft Corp; *type:* fighter; *year:* 1943; *engine:* Pratt & Whitney R-2800-8 Double Wasp 18-cylinder radial air-cooled, 2,000 hp; *wingspan:* 41 ft (12.50 m); *length:* 33 ft 4½ in (10.16 m); *height:* 15 ft 1 in (4.60 m); *weight:* 13,120 lb (5,950 kg) (loaded); *maximum speed:* 417 mph (671 km/h) at 19,900 ft (6,065 m); *ceiling:* 36,900 ft (11,250 m); *range:* 1,015 miles (1,635 km); *armament:* 6 machine guns; *crew:* 1

VOUGHT F4U-1D CORSAIR
Nation: USA; *manufacturer:* United Aircraft Corp; *type:* fighter; *year:* 1944; *engine:* Pratt & Whitney R-2800-8W Double Wasp 18-cylinder radial air-cooled, 2,000 hp; *wingspan:* 41 ft (12.47 m); *length:* 33 ft 4½ in (10.16 m); *height:* 15 ft 1 in (4.60 m); *weight:* 14,000 lb (6,350 kg) (loaded); *maximum speed:* 425 mph (684 km/h) at 20,000 ft (6,100 m); *ceiling:* 37,000 ft (11,280 m); *range:* 1,015 miles (1,635 km); *armament:* 6 machine guns; 2,000 lb (907 kg) of bombs; *crew:* 1

GRUMMAN F6F-3 HELLCAT
Nation: USA; *manufacturer:* Grumman Aircraft Engineering Corp; *type:* fighter; *year:* 1943; *engine:* Pratt & Whitney R-2800-10 Double Wasp 18-cylinder radial air-cooled, 2,000 hp; *wingspan:* 42 ft 10 in (13.06 m); *length:* 33 ft 7 in (10.24 m); *height:* 13 ft 1 in (3.99 m); *weight:* 11,381 lb (5,162 kg) (loaded); *maximum speed:* 376 mph (605 km/h) at 17,300 ft (5,270 m); *ceiling:* 38,400 ft (11,700 m); *range:* 1,090 miles (1,750 km); *armament:* 6 machine guns; *crew:* 1

GRUMMAN F6F-5 HELLCAT
Nation: USA; *manufacturer:* Grumman Aircraft Engineering Corp; *type:* fighter; *year:* 1944; *engine:* Pratt & Whitney R-2800-10W Double Wasp 18-cylinder radial air-cooled, 2,000 hp; *wingspan:* 42 ft 10 in (13.06 m); *length:* 33 ft 7 in (10.24 m); *height:* 13 ft 1 in (3.99 m); *weight:* 15,400 lb (6,970 kg) (loaded); *maximum speed:* 380 mph (610 km/h) at 23,400 ft (7,120 m); *ceiling:* 37,300 ft (11,370 m); *range:* 1,040 miles (1,670 km); *armament:* 6 machine guns; 2,000 lb (907 kg) of bombs; *crew:* 1

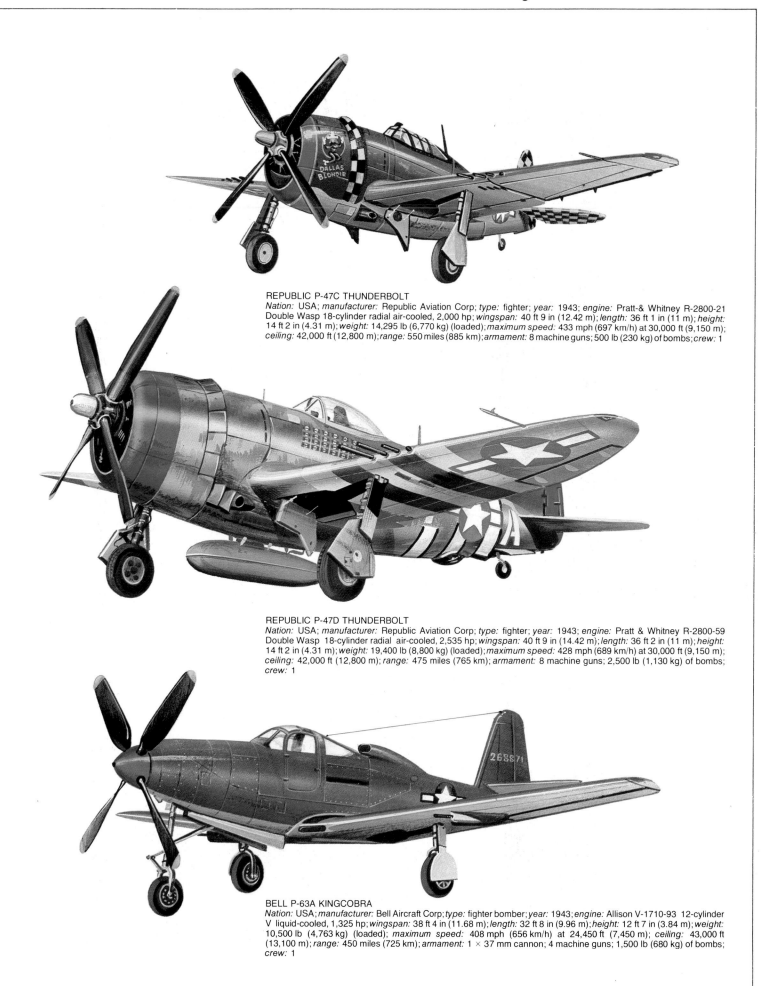

REPUBLIC P-47C THUNDERBOLT
Nation: USA; *manufacturer:* Republic Aviation Corp; *type:* fighter; *year:* 1943; *engine:* Pratt-& Whitney R-2800-21 Double Wasp 18-cylinder radial air-cooled, 2,000 hp; *wingspan:* 40 ft 9 in (12.42 m); *length:* 36 ft 1 in (11 m); *height:* 14 ft 2 in (4.31 m); *weight:* 14,295 lb (6,770 kg) (loaded); *maximum speed:* 433 mph (697 km/h) at 30,000 ft (9,150 m); *ceiling:* 42,000 ft (12,800 m); *range:* 550 miles (885 km); *armament:* 8 machine guns; 500 lb (230 kg) of bombs; *crew:* 1

REPUBLIC P-47D THUNDERBOLT
Nation: USA; *manufacturer:* Republic Aviation Corp; *type:* fighter; *year:* 1943; *engine:* Pratt & Whitney R-2800-59 Double Wasp 18-cylinder radial air-cooled, 2,535 hp; *wingspan:* 40 ft 9 in (14.42 m); *length:* 36 ft 2 in (11 m); *height:* 14 ft 2 in (4.31 m); *weight:* 19,400 lb (8,800 kg) (loaded); *maximum speed:* 428 mph (689 km/h) at 30,000 ft (9,150 m); *ceiling:* 42,000 ft (12,800 m); *range:* 475 miles (765 km); *armament:* 8 machine guns; 2,500 lb (1,130 kg) of bombs; *crew:* 1

BELL P-63A KINGCOBRA
Nation: USA; *manufacturer:* Bell Aircraft Corp; *type:* fighter bomber; *year:* 1943; *engine:* Allison V-1710-93 12-cylinder V liquid-cooled, 1,325 hp; *wingspan:* 38 ft 4 in (11.68 m); *length:* 32 ft 8 in (9.96 m); *height:* 12 ft 7 in (3.84 m); *weight:* 10,500 lb (4,763 kg) (loaded); *maximum speed:* 408 mph (656 km/h) at 24,450 ft (7,450 m); *ceiling:* 43,000 ft (13,100 m); *range:* 450 miles (725 km); *armament:* 1 × 37 mm cannon; 4 machine guns; 1,500 lb (680 kg) of bombs; *crew:* 1

MESSERSCHMITT Me.262A-1a
Nation: Germany; *manufacturer:* Messerschmitt AG; *type:* fighter; *year:* 1944; *engine:* two Junkers Jumo 004B-1, 1,980 lb (898 kg) thrust; *wingspan:* 40 ft 11½ in (12.48 m); *length:* 34 ft 9½ in (10.60 m); *height:* 12 ft 7 in (3.84 m); *weight:* 14,101 lb (6,396 kg) (loaded); *maximum speed:* 540 mph (869 km/h) at 19,685 ft (6,000 m); *ceiling:* 37,565 ft (11,450 m); *range:* 652 miles (1,050 km); *armament:* 4 × 30 mm cannon; *crew:* 1

MESSERSCHMITT Me.163B-1a
Nation: Germany; *manufacturer:* Messerschmitt AG; *type:* interceptor fighter; *year:* 1944; *engine:* Walter HWK 509A-2, 3,750 lb (1,700 kg) thrust; *wingspan:* 30 ft 7 in (9.32 m); *length:* 18 ft 8 in (5.70 m); *height:* 9 ft (2.74 m); *weight:* 8,707 lb (3,950 kg); *maximum speed:* 596 mph (959 km/h); *ceiling:* 39,500 ft (12,039 m); *endurance:* 7½ minutes; *armament:* 2 × 20 mm cannon; *crew:* 1

HEINKEL He.162A-2
Nation: Germany; *manufacturer:* Ernst Heinkel AG; *type:* fighter; *year:* 1945; *engine:* BMW 003E-1 axial-flow turbojet, 1,764 lb (800 kg) thrust; *wingspan:* 23 ft 7½ in (7.20 m); *length:* 29 ft 8 in (9.04 m); *height:* 8 ft 6 in (2.59 m); *weight:* 5,740 lb (2,600 kg) (loaded); *maximum speed:* 521 mph (838 km/h) at 19,690 ft (6,000 m); *ceiling:* 39,400 ft (12,000 m); *range:* 606 miles (975 km); *armament:* 2 × 20 mm cannon; *crew:* 1

BACHEM Ba.349B-1
Nation: Germany; *manufacturer:* Bachem-Werke GmbH; *type:* interceptor fighter; *year:* 1945; *engine:* Walter HWK 509C-1 bi-fuel rocket, 4,400 lb (1,995 kg) thrust; *wingspan:* 13 ft 1½ in (3.39 m); *length:* 19 ft 9 in (6.02 m); *height:* 7 ft 4½ in (2.24 m); *weight:* 4,920 lb (2,230 kg) (loaded); *maximum speed:* 620 mph (997 km/h) at 16,400 ft (5,000 m); *ceiling:* 45,920 ft (13,996 m); *range:* 36¼ miles (58 km); *armament:* 24 × 73 mm rockets; *crew:* 1

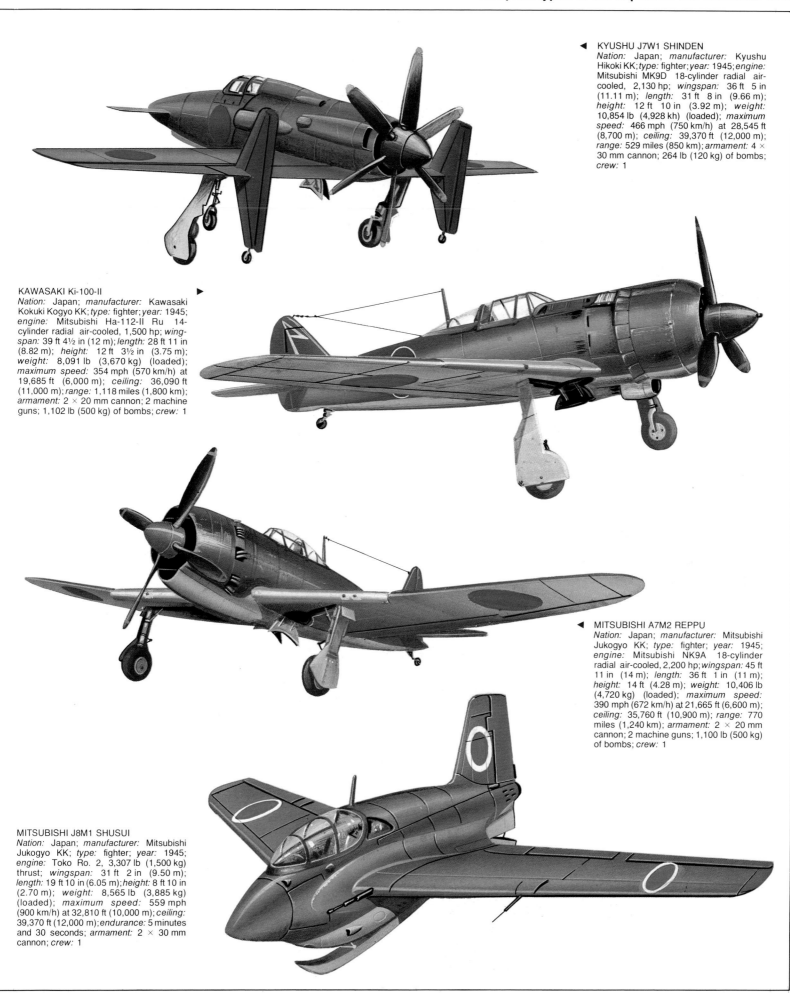

KYUSHU J7W1 SHINDEN
Nation: Japan; manufacturer: Kyushu Hikoki KK; type: fighter; year: 1945; engine: Mitsubishi MK9D 18-cylinder radial air-cooled, 2,130 hp; wingspan: 36 ft 5 in (11.11 m); length: 31 ft 8 in (9.66 m); height: 12 ft 10 in (3.92 m); weight: 10,854 lb (4,928 kh) (loaded); maximum speed: 466 mph (750 km/h) at 28,545 ft (8,700 m); ceiling: 39,370 ft (12,000 m); range: 529 miles (850 km); armament: 4 × 30 mm cannon; 264 lb (120 kg) of bombs; crew: 1

KAWASAKI Ki-100-II
Nation: Japan; manufacturer: Kawasaki Kokuki Kogyo KK; type: fighter; year: 1945; engine: Mitsubishi Ha-112-II Ru 14-cylinder radial air-cooled, 1,500 hp; wingspan: 39 ft 4½ in (12 m); length: 28 ft 11 in (8.82 m); height: 12 ft 3½ in (3.75 m); weight: 8,091 lb (3,670 kg) (loaded); maximum speed: 354 mph (570 km/h) at 19,685 ft (6,000 m); ceiling: 36,090 ft (11,000 m); range: 1,118 miles (1,800 km); armament: 2 × 20 mm cannon; 2 machine guns; 1,102 lb (500 kg) of bombs; crew: 1

MITSUBISHI A7M2 REPPU
Nation: Japan; manufacturer: Mitsubishi Jukogyo KK; type: fighter; year: 1945; engine: Mitsubishi NK9A 18-cylinder radial air-cooled, 2,200 hp; wingspan: 45 ft 11 in (14 m); length: 36 ft 1 in (11 m); height: 14 ft (4.28 m); weight: 10,406 lb (4,720 kg) (loaded); maximum speed: 390 mph (672 km/h) at 21,665 ft (6,600 m); ceiling: 35,760 ft (10,900 m); range: 770 miles (1,240 km); armament: 2 × 20 mm cannon; 2 machine guns; 1,100 lb (500 kg) of bombs; crew: 1

MITSUBISHI J8M1 SHUSUI
Nation: Japan; manufacturer: Mitsubishi Jukogyo KK; type: fighter; year: 1945; engine: Toko Ro. 2, 3,307 lb (1,500 kg) thrust; wingspan: 31 ft 2 in (9.50 m); length: 19 ft 10 in (6.05 m); height: 8 ft 10 in (2.70 m); weight: 8,565 lb (3,885 kg) (loaded); maximum speed: 559 mph (900 km/h) at 32,810 ft (10,000 m); ceiling: 39,370 ft (12,000 m); endurance: 5 minutes and 30 seconds; armament: 2 × 30 mm cannon; crew: 1

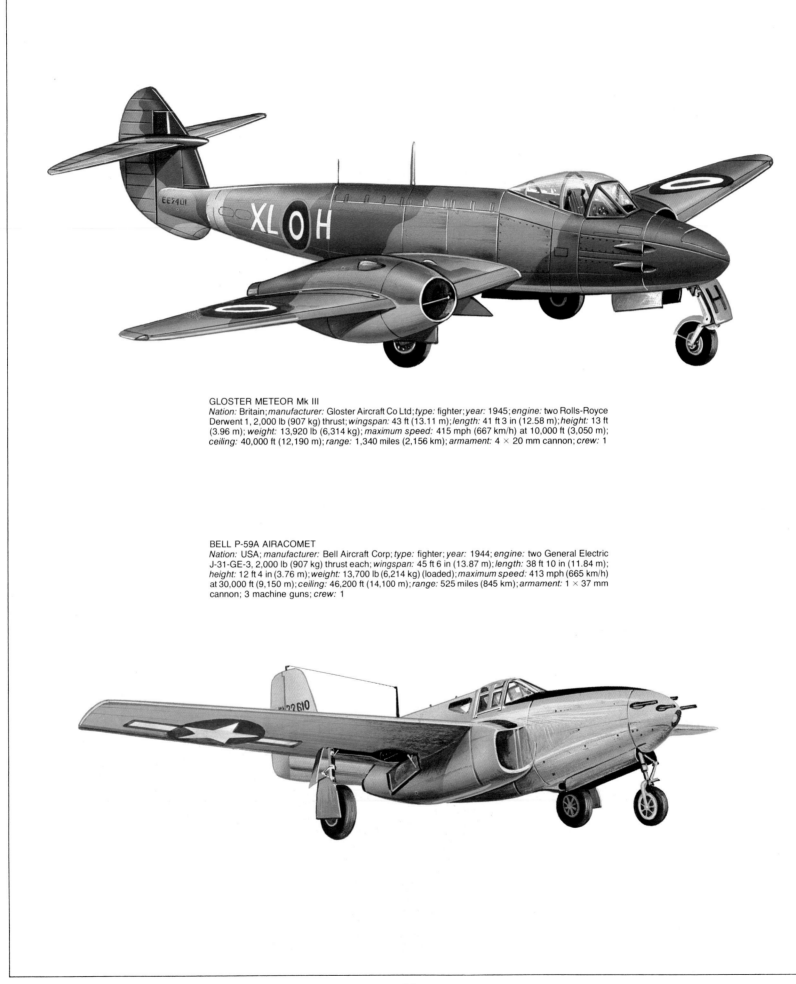

GLOSTER METEOR Mk III
Nation: Britain; *manufacturer:* Gloster Aircraft Co Ltd; *type:* fighter; *year:* 1945; *engine:* two Rolls-Royce Derwent 1, 2,000 lb (907 kg) thrust; *wingspan:* 43 ft (13.11 m); *length:* 41 ft 3 in (12.58 m); *height:* 13 ft (3.96 m); *weight:* 13,920 lb (6,314 kg); *maximum speed:* 415 mph (667 km/h) at 10,000 ft (3,050 m); *ceiling:* 40,000 ft (12,190 m); *range:* 1,340 miles (2,156 km); *armament:* 4 × 20 mm cannon; *crew:* 1

BELL P-59A AIRACOMET
Nation: USA; *manufacturer:* Bell Aircraft Corp; *type:* fighter; *year:* 1944; *engine:* two General Electric J-31-GE-3, 2,000 lb (907 kg) thrust each; *wingspan:* 45 ft 6 in (13.87 m); *length:* 38 ft 10 in (11.84 m); *height:* 12 ft 4 in (3.76 m); *weight:* 13,700 lb (6,214 kg) (loaded); *maximum speed:* 413 mph (665 km/h) at 30,000 ft (9,150 m); *ceiling:* 46,200 ft (14,100 m); *range:* 525 miles (845 km); *armament:* 1 × 37 mm cannon; 3 machine guns; *crew:* 1

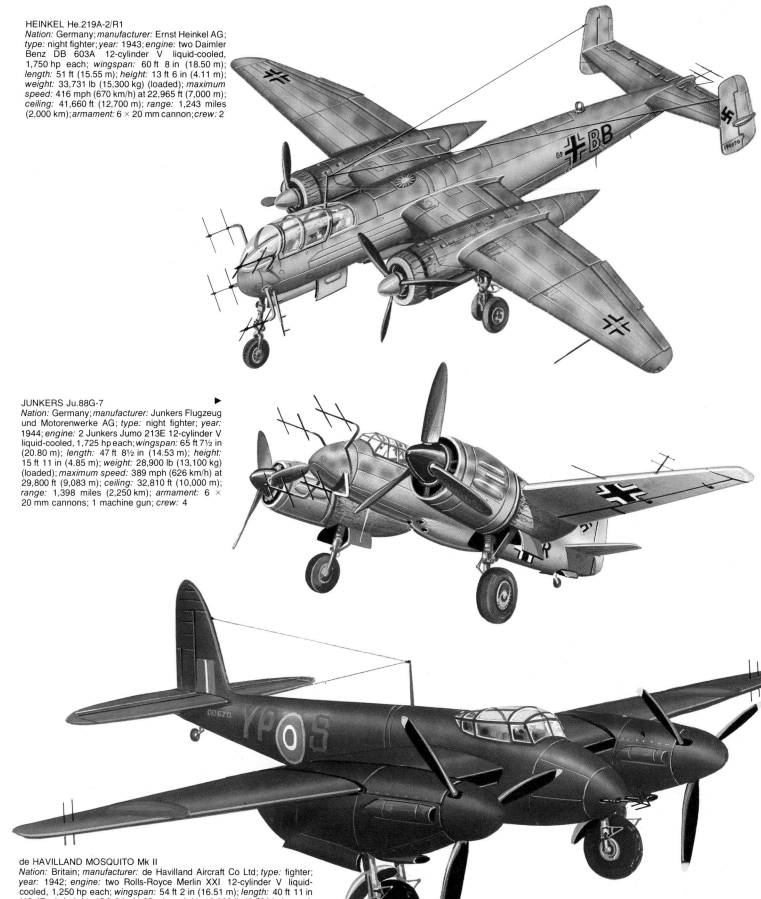

HEINKEL He.219A-2/R1
Nation: Germany; *manufacturer:* Ernst Heinkel AG; *type:* night fighter; *year:* 1943; *engine:* two Daimler Benz DB 603A 12-cylinder V liquid-cooled, 1,750 hp each; *wingspan:* 60 ft 8 in (18.50 m); *length:* 51 ft (15.55 m); *height:* 13 ft 6 in (4.11 m); *weight:* 33,731 lb (15,300 kg) (loaded); *maximum speed:* 416 mph (670 km/h) at 22,965 ft (7,000 m); *ceiling:* 41,660 ft (12,700 m); *range:* 1,243 miles (2,000 km); *armament:* 6 × 20 mm cannon; *crew:* 2

JUNKERS Ju.88G-7 ▶
Nation: Germany; *manufacturer:* Junkers Flugzeug und Motorenwerke AG; *type:* night fighter; *year:* 1944; *engine:* 2 Junkers Jumo 213E 12-cylinder V liquid-cooled, 1,725 hp each; *wingspan:* 65 ft 7½ in (20.80 m); *length:* 47 ft 8½ in (14.53 m); *height:* 15 ft 11 in (4.85 m); *weight:* 28,900 lb (13,100 kg) (loaded); *maximum speed:* 389 mph (626 km/h) at 29,800 ft (9,083 m); *ceiling:* 32,810 ft (10,000 m); *range:* 1,398 miles (2,250 km); *armament:* 6 × 20 mm cannons; 1 machine gun; *crew:* 4

de HAVILLAND MOSQUITO Mk II
Nation: Britain; *manufacturer:* de Havilland Aircraft Co Ltd; *type:* fighter; *year:* 1942; *engine:* two Rolls-Royce Merlin XXI 12-cylinder V liquid-cooled, 1,250 hp each; *wingspan:* 54 ft 2 in (16.51 m); *length:* 40 ft 11 in (12.47 m); *height:* 15 ft 3 in (4.65 m); *weight:* 18,800 lb (8,528 kg); *maximum speed:* 356 mph (572 km/h) at 9,000 ft (2,745 m); *ceiling:* 34,500 ft (10,500 m); *range:* 1,520 miles (2,445 km); *armament:* 4 × 20 mm cannon; 4 machine guns; *crew:* 2

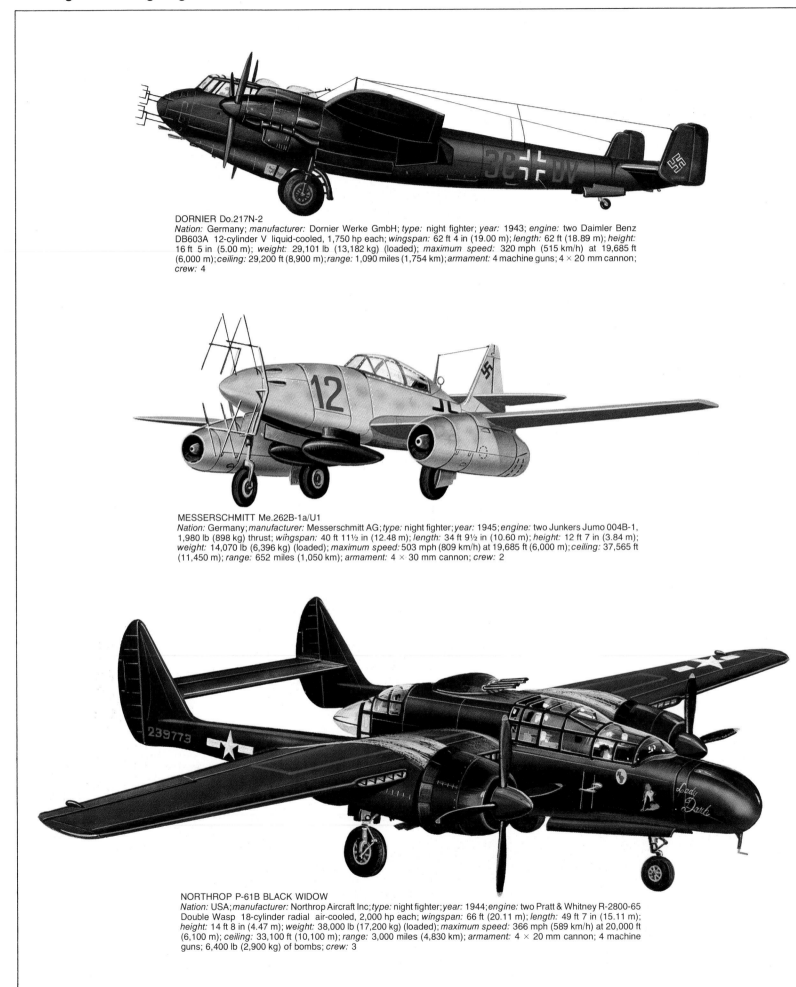

DORNIER Do.217N-2
Nation: Germany; *manufacturer:* Dornier Werke GmbH; *type:* night fighter; *year:* 1943; *engine:* two Daimler Benz DB603A 12-cylinder V liquid-cooled, 1,750 hp each; *wingspan:* 62 ft 4 in (19.00 m); *length:* 62 ft (18.89 m); *height:* 16 ft 5 in (5.00 m); *weight:* 29,101 lb (13,182 kg) (loaded); *maximum speed:* 320 mph (515 km/h) at 19,685 ft (6,000 m); *ceiling:* 29,200 ft (8,900 m); *range:* 1,090 miles (1,754 km); *armament:* 4 machine guns; 4 × 20 mm cannon; *crew:* 4

MESSERSCHMITT Me.262B-1a/U1
Nation: Germany; *manufacturer:* Messerschmitt AG; *type:* night fighter; *year:* 1945; *engine:* two Junkers Jumo 004B-1, 1,980 lb (898 kg) thrust; *wingspan:* 40 ft 11½ in (12.48 m); *length:* 34 ft 9½ in (10.60 m); *height:* 12 ft 7 in (3.84 m); *weight:* 14,070 lb (6,396 kg) (loaded); *maximum speed:* 503 mph (809 km/h) at 19,685 ft (6,000 m); *ceiling:* 37,565 ft (11,450 m); *range:* 652 miles (1,050 km); *armament:* 4 × 30 mm cannon; *crew:* 2

NORTHROP P-61B BLACK WIDOW
Nation: USA; *manufacturer:* Northrop Aircraft Inc; *type:* night fighter; *year:* 1944; *engine:* two Pratt & Whitney R-2800-65 Double Wasp 18-cylinder radial air-cooled, 2,000 hp each; *wingspan:* 66 ft (20.11 m); *length:* 49 ft 7 in (15.11 m); *height:* 14 ft 8 in (4.47 m); *weight:* 38,000 lb (17,200 kg) (loaded); *maximum speed:* 366 mph (589 km/h) at 20,000 ft (6,100 m); *ceiling:* 33,100 ft (10,100 m); *range:* 3,000 miles (4,830 km); *armament:* 4 × 20 mm cannon; 4 machine guns; 6,400 lb (2,900 kg) of bombs; *crew:* 3

HENSCHEL Hs 123A-1
Nation: Germany; *manufacturer:* Henschel Flugzeugw. AG;
type: ground-attack fighter; *year:* 1936; *engine:* BMW 132
Dc 9-cylinder radial air-cooled, 880 hp; *wingspan:* 34 ft
5 in (10.50 m); *length:* 27 ft 4 in (8.33 m); *height:* 10 ft 6 in
(3.21 m); *weight:* 4,888 lb (2,200 kg) (loaded); *maximum
speed:* 212 mph (317 km/h) at 3,940 ft (1,200 m); *ceiling:*
29,525 ft (9,000 m); *range:* 534 miles (860 km); *armament:*
2 machine guns; 440 lb (200 kg) of bombs; *crew:* 1 ►

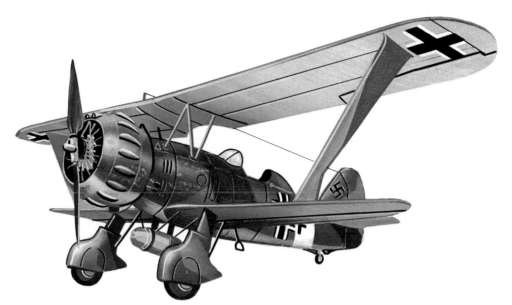

HENSCHEL Hs 129B-1
Nation: Germany; *manufacturer:* Henschel Flugzeugw. AG;
type: ground attack; *year:* 1942; *engine:* two Gnome-Rhône
14M 14-cylinder radial air-cooled, 700 hp each; *wingspan:*
46 ft 7 in (14.20 m); *length:* 32 ft (9.73 m); *height:* 10 ft 8 in
(3.25 m); *weight:* 11,574 lb (5,243 kg) (loaded); *maximum
speed:* 253 mph (407 km/h) at 12,570 ft (3,800 m); *ceiling:*
29,530 ft (9,000 m); *range:* 428 miles (690 km); *armament:*
6 machine guns; 2 × 20 mm cannon; 1 × 30 mm cannon;
crew: 1 ▼

ILYUSHIN Il-10
Nation: USSR; *manufacturer:* State Industries; *type:* attack;
year: 1944; *engine:* Mikulin AM-42 12-cylinder V liquid-
cooled, 2,000 hp; *wingspan:* 43 ft 11½ in (13.54 m); *length:*
36 ft 9 in (11.30 m); *height:* 11 ft 6 in (3.50 m); *weight:*
14,409 lb (6,550 kg) (loaded); *maximum speed:* 311 mph
(550 km/h); *ceiling:* 24,606 ft (7,570 m); *range:* 621 miles
(1,000 km); *armament:* 3 × 20 mm cannon; 2 machine
guns; *crew:* 2
▼

▲ YAKOVLEV Yak-3
Nation: USSR; *manufacturer:* State Industries; *type:* attack fighter; *year:* 1944;
engine: Klimov M-105PF-2 12-cylinder V
liquid-cooled, 1,300 hp; *wingspan:* 30 ft
2 in (9.20 m); *length:* 27 ft 11 in (8.50 m);
height: 7 ft 11 in (2.40 m); *weight:* 5,864 lb
(2,660 kg) (loaded); *maximum speed:*
403 mph (648 km/h) at 16,400 ft (5,000 m);
ceiling: 35,430 ft (10,900 m); *range:* 560
miles (900 km); *armament:* 1 × 20 mm
cannon; 2 machine guns; *crew:* 1

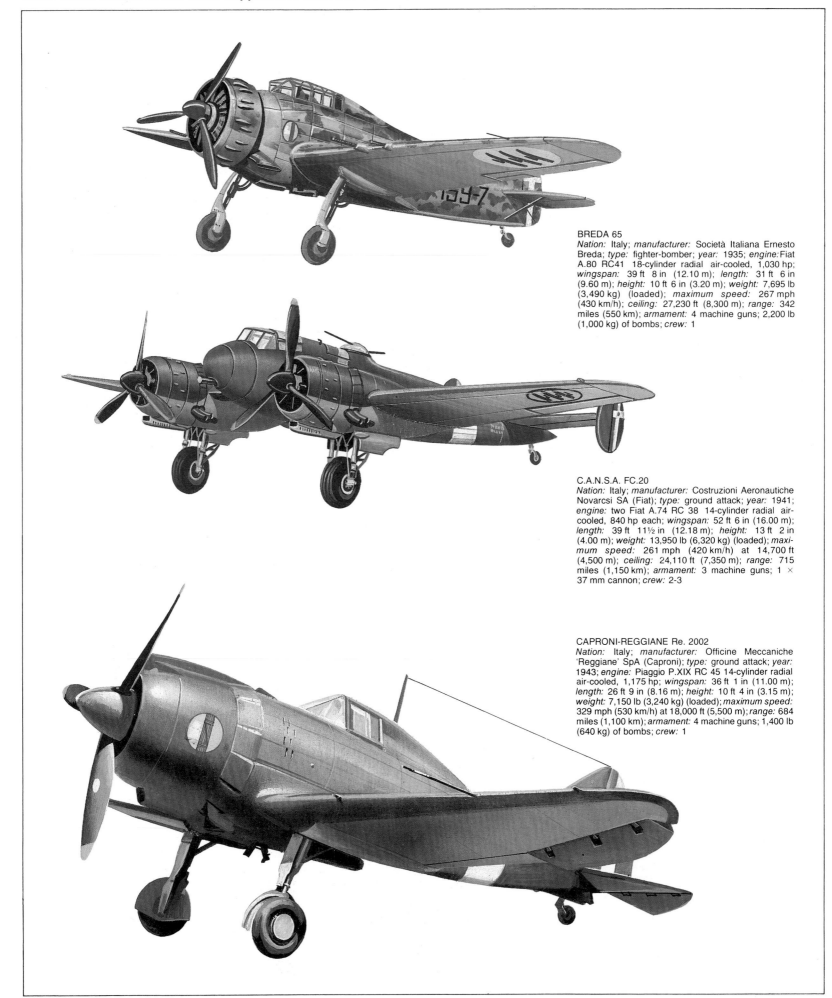

BREDA 65
Nation: Italy; *manufacturer:* Società Italiana Ernesto Breda; *type:* fighter-bomber; *year:* 1935; *engine:* Fiat A.80 RC41 18-cylinder radial air-cooled, 1,030 hp; *wingspan:* 39 ft 8 in (12.10 m); *length:* 31 ft 6 in (9.60 m); *height:* 10 ft 6 in (3.20 m); *weight:* 7,695 lb (3,490 kg) (loaded); *maximum speed:* 267 mph (430 km/h); *ceiling:* 27,230 ft (8,300 m); *range:* 342 miles (550 km); *armament:* 4 machine guns; 2,200 lb (1,000 kg) of bombs; *crew:* 1

C.A.N.S.A. FC.20
Nation: Italy; *manufacturer:* Costruzioni Aeronautiche Novarcsi SA (Fiat) *type:* ground attack; *year:* 1941; *engine:* two Fiat A.74 RC 38 14-cylinder radial air-cooled, 840 hp each; *wingspan:* 52 ft 6 in (16.00 m); *length:* 39 ft 11½ in (12.18 m); *height:* 13 ft 2 in (4.00 m); *weight:* 13,950 lb (6,320 kg) (loaded); *maximum speed:* 261 mph (420 km/h) at 14,700 ft (4,500 m); *ceiling:* 24,110 ft (7,350 m); *range:* 715 miles (1,150 km); *armament:* 3 machine guns; 1 × 37 mm cannon; *crew:* 2-3

CAPRONI-REGGIANE Re. 2002
Nation: Italy; *manufacturer:* Officine Meccaniche 'Reggiane' SpA (Caproni); *type:* ground attack; *year:* 1943; *engine:* Piaggio P.XIX RC 45 14-cylinder radial air-cooled, 1,175 hp; *wingspan:* 36 ft 1 in (11.00 m); *length:* 26 ft 9 in (8.16 m); *height:* 10 ft 4 in (3.15 m); *weight:* 7,150 lb (3,240 kg) (loaded); *maximum speed:* 329 mph (530 km/h) at 18,000 ft (5,500 m); *range:* 684 miles (1,100 km); *armament:* 4 machine guns; 1,400 lb (640 kg) of bombs; *crew:* 1

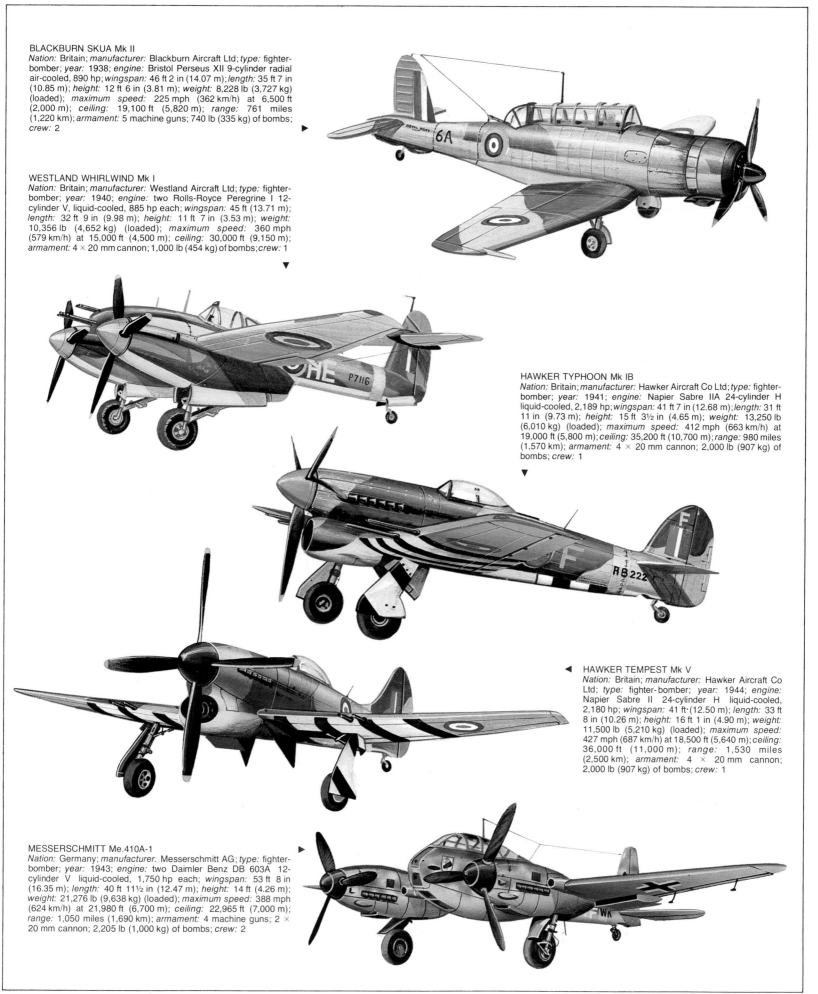

BLACKBURN SKUA Mk II
Nation: Britain; *manufacturer:* Blackburn Aircraft Ltd; *type:* fighter-bomber; *year:* 1938; *engine:* Bristol Perseus XII 9-cylinder radial air-cooled, 890 hp; *wingspan:* 46 ft 2 in (14.07 m); *length:* 35 ft 7 in (10.85 m); *height:* 12 ft 6 in (3.81 m); *weight:* 8,228 lb (3,727 kg) (loaded); *maximum speed:* 225 mph (362 km/h) at 6,500 ft (2,000 m); *ceiling:* 19,100 ft (5,820 m); *range:* 761 miles (1,220 km); *armament:* 5 machine guns; 740 lb (335 kg) of bombs; *crew:* 2

WESTLAND WHIRLWIND Mk I
Nation: Britain; *manufacturer:* Westland Aircraft Ltd; *type:* fighter-bomber; *year:* 1940; *engine:* two Rolls-Royce Peregrine I 12-cylinder V, liquid-cooled, 885 hp each; *wingspan:* 45 ft (13.71 m); *length:* 32 ft 9 in (9.98 m); *height:* 11 ft 7 in (3.53 m); *weight:* 10,356 lb (4,652 kg) (loaded); *maximum speed:* 360 mph (579 km/h) at 15,000 ft (4,500 m); *ceiling:* 30,000 ft (9,150 m); *armament:* 4 × 20 mm cannon; 1,000 lb (454 kg) of bombs; *crew:* 1

HAWKER TYPHOON Mk IB
Nation: Britain; *manufacturer:* Hawker Aircraft Co Ltd; *type:* fighter-bomber; *year:* 1941; *engine:* Napier Sabre IIA 24-cylinder H liquid-cooled, 2,189 hp; *wingspan:* 41 ft 7 in (12.68 m); *length:* 31 ft 11 in (9.73 m); *height:* 15 ft 3½ in (4.65 m); *weight:* 13,250 lb (6,010 kg) (loaded); *maximum speed:* 412 mph (663 km/h) at 19,000 ft (5,800 m); *ceiling:* 35,200 ft (10,700 m); *range:* 980 miles (1,570 km); *armament:* 4 × 20 mm cannon; 2,000 lb (907 kg) of bombs; *crew:* 1

HAWKER TEMPEST Mk V
Nation: Britain; *manufacturer:* Hawker Aircraft Co Ltd; *type:* fighter-bomber; *year:* 1944; *engine:* Napier Sabre II 24-cylinder H liquid-cooled, 2,180 hp; *wingspan:* 41 ft (12.50 m); *length:* 33 ft 8 in (10.26 m); *height:* 16 ft 1 in (4.90 m); *weight:* 11,500 lb (5,210 kg) (loaded); *maximum speed:* 427 mph (687 km/h) at 18,500 ft (5,640 m); *ceiling:* 36,000 ft (11,000 m); *range:* 1,530 miles (2,500 km); *armament:* 4 × 20 mm cannon; 2,000 lb (907 kg) of bombs; *crew:* 1

MESSERSCHMITT Me.410A-1
Nation: Germany; *manufacturer:* Messerschmitt AG; *type:* fighter-bomber; *year:* 1943; *engine:* two Daimler Benz DB 603A 12-cylinder V liquid-cooled, 1,750 hp each; *wingspan:* 53 ft 8 in (16.35 m); *length:* 40 ft 11½ in (12.47 m); *height:* 14 ft (4.26 m); *weight:* 21,276 lb (9,638 kg) (loaded); *maximum speed:* 388 mph (624 km/h) at 21,980 ft (6,700 m); *ceiling:* 22,965 ft (7,000 m); *range:* 1,050 miles (1,690 km); *armament:* 4 machine guns; 2 × 20 mm cannon; 2,205 lb (1,000 kg) of bombs; *crew:* 2

BRISTOL MERCURY - 1927 (GB)
A derivant of the Jupiter engine of 1920, the Mercury was a 9-cylinder radial engine with reduction gear. The maximum power which could be sustained for 5 minutes of level flight ranged according to the different variants between 840 hp and 995 hp at 2,750 rpm. Power at take-off however was between 725 hp and 905 hp at 2,650 rpm. The capacity of the engine was 24.9 litres, its diameter 130 cm and the dry weight was 1,066 lb (483.5 kg). Between 1939 and 1945 20,700 Mercury engines were constructed in a number ◀ of variants

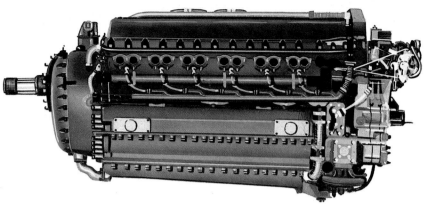

ALLISON V-1710 - 1932 (USA)
The production series of this V-12 liquid-cooled engine, developed from 1930, was one of the oldest and most widely used American engines. The Allison engines were never, however, particularly outstanding power units, especially at high altitude. Total capacity of this 12-cylinder engine was 29 litres. In the last production series, power at take-off varied between 1,200 hp and 1,475 hp at 3,000 rpm; its dry weight varied between 1,386 lb (628.8 kg) and 1,622 lb (735.5 kg)

PRATT & WHITNEY R 1830 TWIN WASP - 1930 (USA)
A 14-cylinder double bank radial engine of 1,200 hp. Large numbers were produced. It had a capacity of 30 litres and could be fitted with various types of supercharger. The diameter was 122.2 cm and dry weight varied between 1,437 lb (652 kg) and 1,460 lb (667 kg)

ROLLS-ROYCE MERLIN - 1936 (GB)
Probably the most famous engine of the war was the Merlin, of which 150,000 were constructed and were used in all the most important British aircraft of the war. It was a 12-cylinder, V-type liquid-cooled engine of 27 litres capacity with a supercharger and weighed between 1,375 lb (624 kg) and 1,650 lb (749 kg). The 1,030 hp of the Merlin was increased to 2,000 hp in the later versions.

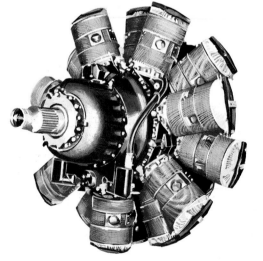

BRISTOL HERCULES - 1936 (GB)
During the war 57,500 of these engines were produced in various types. It was a 14-cylinder double-bank radial engine in which power progressed from the initial 1,375 hp to 1,800 hp. Its capacity was 38.7 litres and it was supercharged. Diameter was 132 cm, weight between 1,872 lb (849 kg) and 1,991 lb (903 kg)

NAKAJIMA SAKAE - 1939 (J)
One of the most famous and widely used Japanese engines, which powered the Mitsubishi A6M Reisen, the well-known Zero fighter. The Sakae was a 14-cylinder double-bank radial engine with supercharger and its top performance varied between 1,100 and 1,200 hp. Total capacity was 27.8 litres, diameter 114.4 cm and its weight only just over 1,175 lb (533 kg)

JUNKERS JUMO 211 - 1938 (G)
An inverted V-12 liquid-cooled engine with supercharger and fuel injection. Total capacity was 35 litres, dry weight 640 kg. Many variants were manufactured, and power rose from 950 hp at 2,200 rpm in the type A to 1,500 hp at 2,700 rpm in the Q series.

PRATT & WHITNEY R-2800 DOUBLE WASP - 1939 (USA)
The series R-2800 developed from the earlier Wasp radial engines was one of the most outstanding power units in the 2,000 hp range. The Double Wasp was an 18-cylinder double bank radial engine. Total capacity was 45.9 litres, with supercharger and reduction gear.

BMW 801 - 1940 (G)
The BMW was one of the best radial engines produced by German industry and became famous for its high performance. It was a 14-cylinder double bank radial engine with supercharger and fuel injection. Power increased from 1,600 hp at 2,700 rpm in the earlier series to about 2,300 hp at 2,700 rpm in the latest series. Total capacity was 41.8 litres, diameter varied between 129 cm and 144 cm and dry weight rose from 1,055 kg in the 801 C model to 1,800 kg in the type R.

WRIGHT R-3350 CYCLONE - 1940 (USA)
The R-3350 became one of the best-known engines in the 2,200 hp range. It was an 18-cylinder double bank radial with supercharger and reduction gear. Total capacity was 54.56 litres; diameter 142 cm; dry weight approximately 1,200 kg. Maximum power of 2,200 hp was produced at 2,800 rpm

ROLLS-ROYCE GRIFFON - 1942 (GB)
This was a V-12 liquid-cooled engine, supercharged by a single- or two-stage, two-speed compressor. Total capacity was 36.7 litres, dry weight rose from 816 kg in the early single-stage compressor models to 898 kg in the last models with a two-stage compressor. Power rose from 1,730 hp to 2,300 hp in the last models.
▼

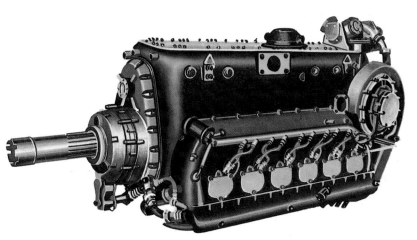

DAIMLER BENZ DB 605 - 1941 (G)
During the war Daimler Benz produced in the greatest numbers German's most widely used aircraft engines; the DB 605 was an inverted V-12 liquid-cooled engine with fuel injection and supercharger. Power was 1,475 hp at 2,800 rpm on take-off. Dry weight was approximately 756 kg. In the last types, power rose to 2,000 hp

Fighter production in the Second World War

	Legend
Britain	▬
Germany	▬
Italy	▬
France	▬
United States	▬
USSR	▬
Japan	▬

527 Gloster Gladiator
602 Fairey Fulmar
614 Bloch MB-152
658 Fairey Firefly
700 Northrop P.61 Black Widow
775 Dewoitine D.520
782 Fiat G.50
800 Hawker Tempest
1064 Boulton Paul Defiant
1081 Morane-Saulnier M.S. 406
1094 Mitsubishi A5M
1100 Macchi M.C.202
1100 Potez 630
1151 Macchi M.C.200
1160 Messerschmitt Me.410
1225 Nakajima Ki-44 Shoki
1430 Messerschmitt Me.262
1435 Kawanishi N1K1-J Shiden
1701 Kawasaki Ki-45 Toryu
1781 Fiat C.R.42
2089 Supermarine Seafire
2100 Mikoyan-Gurevich MIG-1
3303 Bell P-63 Kingcobra
3078 Kawasaki Ki-61 Hien
3330 Hawker Typhoon
3399 Nakajima Ki-27
3514 Nakajima Ki-84 Hayate
5562 Bristol Beaufighter
5919 Nakajima Ki-43 Hayabusa
6050 Messerschmitt Bf.110
8000 Grumman F4F Wildcat
9558 Bell P-39 Airacobra
9923 Lockheed P-38 Lightning
10.449 Mitsubishi A6M Reisen
12.272 Grumman F6F Hellcat
12.681 Vought F4U Corsair
13.733 Curtiss P-40 Warhawk
14.233 Hawker Hurricane
15.000 Lavochkin La-5
15.683 Republic P-47 Thunderbolt
15.686 North American P-51 Mustang
20.000 Polikarpov I-16
20.001 Focke Wulf Fw.190
20.351 Supermarine Spitfire
30.000 Yakovlev Yak-1
35.000 Messerschmitt Bf.109

0 1000 2 3 4 5 6 7 8 9 10.000 11 12 13 14 15 16 17 18 19 20.000 21 22 23 24 25 26 27 28 29 30.000 31 32 33 34 35

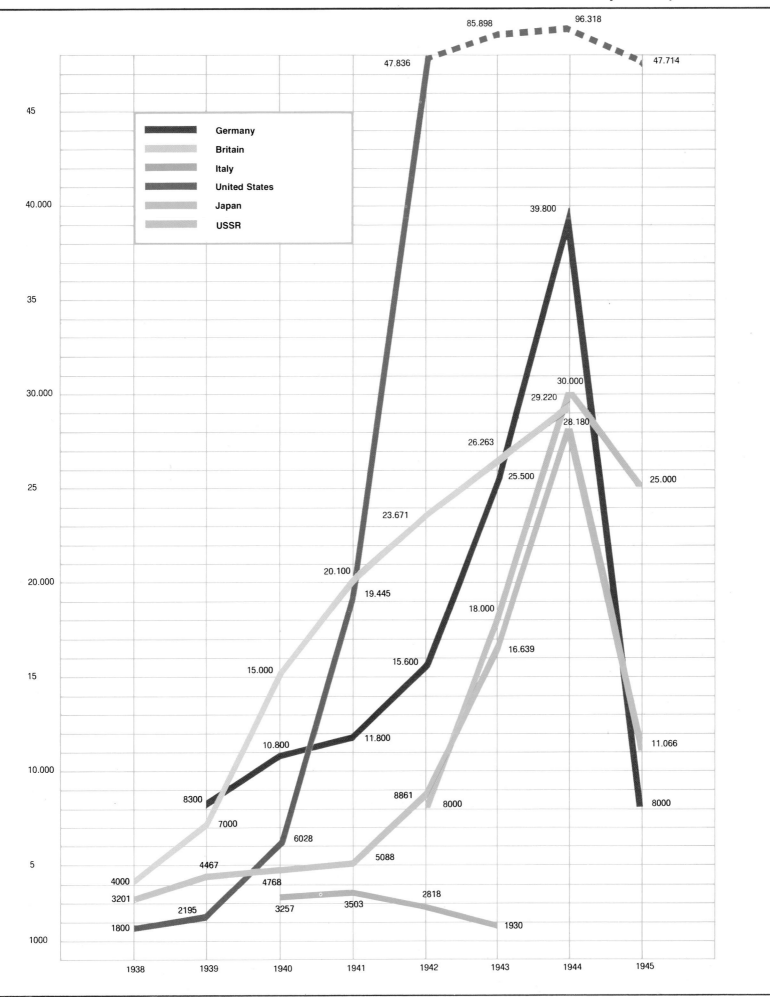

Comparative analysis of speeds of Second World War fighters

Legend	
1935	(black)
1937	(light grey)
1938	(grey)
1939	(dark grey)
1940	(grey)
1941	(light grey)
1942	(grey)
1943	(dark grey)
1944	(dark grey)
1945	(black)

Avia B.534 (CS)

Gloster Gladiator Mk.I (GB)

PZL P.24 (PL)

Mitsubishi A5M4 (J)

Fiat C.R.42 (I)

Seversky P-35 (USA)

Fokker D.XXI (NL)

Polikarpov I-16/10 (USSR)

Nakajima Ki-27 (J)

Fiat G.50 (I)

Fokker G-1A (NL)

Morane-Saulnier M.S.406 (F)

Commonwealth CA-12 Boomerang (AUS)

Caudron C.714 (F)

Polikarpov I-17 (USSR)

Kawanishi N1K1 Kyofu (J)

Nakajima Ki-43-Ia (J)

Curtiss P-36C (USA)

Fairey Firefly Mk.I (GB)

I.A.R. 80 (R)

Macchi M.C.200 (I)

Bloch MB-152 (F)

Bristol Beaufighter Mk.IF (GB)

Brewster F2A-3 Buffalo (USA)

Hawker Hurricane Mk.I (GB)

Rogozarski IK-3 (YU)

Dewoitine D.520 (F)

Reggiane Re.2000 (I)

Reggiane Re.2002 (I)

Nakajima Ki-43-IIb (J)

Grumman F4F-3 Wildcat (USA)

Mitsubishi A6M2 Reisen (J)

Messerschmitt Bf.110 C-1 (G)

Kawasaki Ki-45 KAIa Toryu (J)

Messerschmitt Bf.109 E-1 (G)

Lavochkin LaGG-3 (USSR)

Republic P-43A Lancer (USA)

Reggiane Re.2001 (I)

Curtiss P-40B Warhawk (USA)

Kawasaki Ki-100--II (J)

km/h 300   400   500   600   700   800   900   1000

Supermarine Spitfire Mk.I (GB)
Kawasaki Ki-102a (J)
Kawanishi N1K1-J Shiden (J)
Yakovlev Yak-1 (USSR)
Mitsubishi J2M3 Raiden (J)
Northrop P-61B Black Widow (USA)
Kawasaki Ki-61-I Hien (J)
Bell P-39D Airacobra (USA)
Mikoyan-Gurevich MiG-5 (USSR)
Yakovlev Yak-9D (USSR)
Macchi M.C.202 (I)
Grumman F6F-3 Hellcat (USA)
Nakajima Ki-44-IIb Shoki (J)
Curtiss P-40N (USA)
Focke Wulf Fw.190 A-3 (G)
Fiat G.55 (I)
Focke Wulf Fw.190 A-1 (G)
Mikoyan-Gurevich MiG-1 (USSR)
North American P-51A Mustang (USA)
Nakajima Ki-84-Ia Hayate (J)
Lockheed P-38F Lightning (USA)
Lavochkin La-5FN (USSR)
Macchi M.C.205 (I)
Mikoyan-Gurevich MiG-3 (USSR)
Bell P-63A Kingcobra (USA)
Heinkel He.219 A-2/R1 (G)
Vought F4U-1 Corsair (USA)
Reggiane Re.2005 (I)
Lavochkin La-7 (USSR)
Mikoyan-Gurevich MiG-7 (USSR)
Republic P-47 Thunderbolt (USA)
North American P-51D (USA)
Supermarine Spitfire Mk.XIV (GB)
Messerschmitt Bf.109 K-4 (G)
Gloster Meteor Mk.III (GB)
Heinkel He.162 A-2 (G)
Messerschmitt Me.262 A-1a (G)
Messerschmitt Me.163 B-1a (G)

300   400   500   600   700   800   900   1000

Comparative analysis of ranges of Second World War fighters

Curtiss P-40N Warhawk (USA)

Ikarus IK-2 (YU)

Rogozarski IK-3 (YU)

Messerschmitt Bf.109 K-4 (G)

Mikoyan-Gurevich MiG-1 (USSR)

Bloch MB-152 (F)

Avia B-534 (CS)

Nakajima Ki-27 (J)

Lavochkin La-7 (USSR)

Lavochkin LaGG-3 (USSR)

Messerschmitt Bf.109 E-1 (G)

Fiat G.50 (I)

Gloster Gladiator Mk.I (GB)

Yakovlev Yak-1 (USSR)

Lavochkin La-5FN (USSR)

Lockheed P-38F Lightning (USA)

Bell P-63A Kingcobra (USA)

Supermarine Spitfire Mk.XIV (GB)

Macchi M.C.202 (I)

Fiat C.R.42 (I)

Focke Wulf Fw.190 A-1 (G)

Focke Wulf Fw.190 A-3 (G)

PZL P.24 (PL)

Morane-Saulnier M.S.406 (F)

Polikarpov I-16/10 (USSR)

Polikarpov I-17 (USSR)

Supermarine Spitfire Mk.I (GB)

Mikoyan-Gurevich MiG-3 (USSR)

Hawker Hurricane Mk.I (GB)

Macchi M.C.200 (I)

Republic P-47 Thunderbolt (USA)

Caudron C.714 (F)

Fokker D.XXI (NL)

I.A.R. 80 (R)

Heinkel He.162 A-2 (G)

Dewoitine D.520 (F)

Macchi M.C.205 (I)

Messerschmitt Me.262 A-1a (G)

Reggiane Re.2001 (I)

Reggiane Re.2002 (I)

1935	
1937	
1938	
1939	
1940	
1941	
1942	
1943	
1944	
1945	

km 300 4 5 6 7 8 9 1000 11 12 13 14 15 16 17 18 19 2000 21 22 23 24 25 26

Kawasaki Ki-61-I Hien (J)

Messerschmitt Bf.110 C-1 (G)

North American P-51A Mustang (USA)

Mitsubishi A5M4 (J)

Nakajima Ki-43-Ia (J)

Potez 630 (F)

Reggiane Re.2005 (I)

Bell P-39D Airacobra (USA)

Republic P-43A Lancer (USA)

Yakovlev Yak-9D (USSR)

Curtiss P-36C (USA)

Grumman F4F-3 Wildcat (USA)

Reggiane Re.2000 (I)

Curtiss P-40B Warhawk (USA)

Commonwealth CA-12 Boomerang (AUS)

Fokker G-1A (NL)

North American P-51D Mustang (USA)

Brewster F2A-3 Buffalo (USA)

Vought F4U-1 Corsair (USA)

Fiat G.55 (I)

Kawanishi N1K1 Kyofu (J)

Nakajima Ki-84-Ia Hayate (J)

Nakajima Ki-44-IIb Shoki (J)

Grumman F6F-3 Hellcat (USA)

Nakajima Ki-43-IIb (J)

Kawasaki Ki-100-II (J)

Seversky P-35 (USA)

Bristol Beaufighter Mk.IF (GB)

Mitsubishi J2M3 Raiden (J)

Kawasaki Ki-102a (J)

Heinkel He.219 A-2/R1 (G)

Fairey Firefly Mk.I (GB)

Gloster Meteor Mk.III (GB)

Kawasaki Ki-45 KAIa Toryu (J)

Kawanishi N1K1-J Shiden (J)

300   4   5   6   7   8   9   1000   11   12   13   14   15   16   17   18   19   2000   21   22   23   24   25   26

Fairey Swordfish-1936, GB

Gloster Gladiator-1937, GB

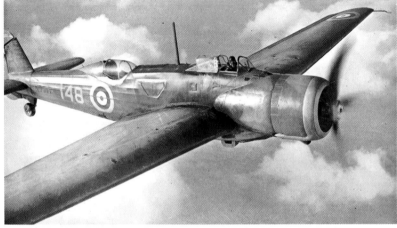

Vickers Wellesley-1937, GB

Westland Lysander-1938, GB

Vickers Wellington-1938, GB

de Havilland Tiger Moth-1938, GB

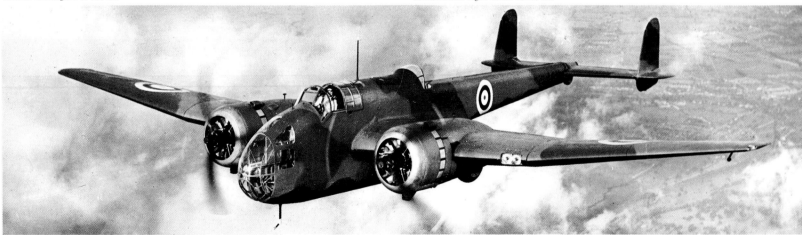

Handley Page Hampden-1938, GB

Short Sunderland-1938, GB & Short Stirling-1940, GB

Supermarine Spitfire-1940, GB

Bristol Beaufighter-1940, GB

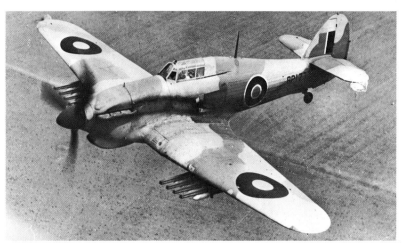

Hawker Hurricane-1941, GB

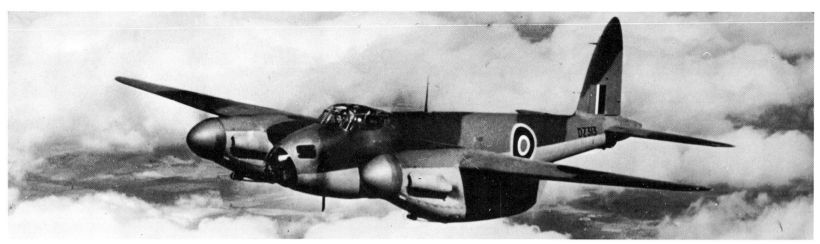

de Havilland Mosquito-1941, GB

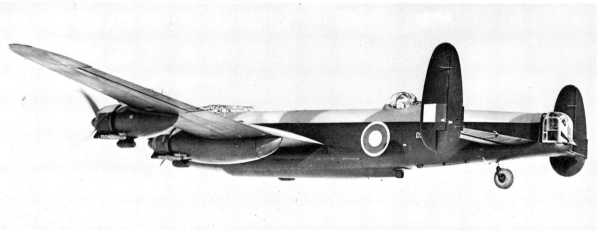

Hawker Typhoon-1941, GB

Avro Lancaster-1942, GB

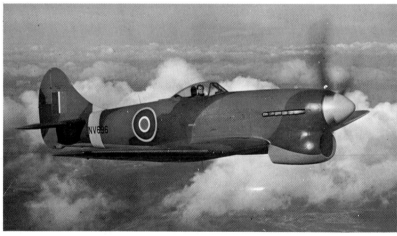

Armstrong Whitworth Albemarle-1943, GB

Hawker Tempest-1944, GB

Bloch 210-1935, F

Dewoitine D.520-1943, F

Morane-Saulnier M.S.406-1938, F

Lioré et Olivier LeO.45-1939, F

Potez 63-1940, F

Junkers Ju.52-1934, G

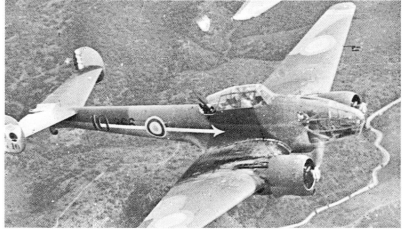

Junkers Ju.87 B-1-1938, G

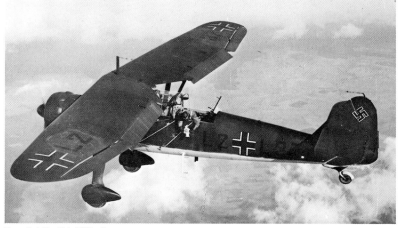

Henschel Hs.126-1939, G

Heinkel He.111-1939, G

Messerschmitt Bf.110-1939, G

Fieseler Fi.156-1939, G

Focke Wulf Fw.189-1940, G

Dornier Do.217-1940, G

Blohm und Voss Bv.141-1940, G

Dornier Do.24-1940, G

Blohm und Voss Bv.138-1941, G

Blohm und Voss Bv.222-1942, G (plate 154)

Blohm und Voss Bv.222-1942, G

54

Messerschmitt Me.323-1942, G

Messerschmitt Bf.109-1942, G

Junkers Ju.290-1942, G

Focke Wulf Fw.190-1942, G

Heinkel He.219-1943, G

55

Messerschmitt Me.410-1943, G

Dornier Do.335-1944, G

Messerschmitt Me.262-1944, G

Messerschmitt Me.163B-1-1944, G

Heinkel He.162-1945, G

CANT Z.501-1934, I

Breda Ba.65-1935, I

SIAI Marchetti S.M.81-1935, I

SIAI Marchetti S.M.79-1936, I

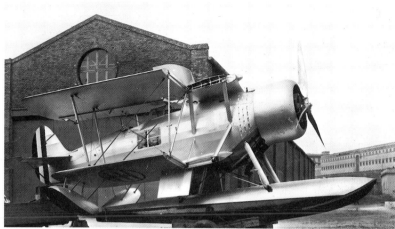

Imam Ro.43-1936, I

CANT Z.506-1937, I

CANT Z.1007 bis-1938, I

Fiat B.R.20-1938, I

Fiat C.R.42-1939, I

SIAI Marchetti S.M.82-1940, I

Fiat G.50-1939, I

Piaggio P.108-1942, I

Macchi M.C.202-1941, I

Fiat G.55-1942, I

Reggiane Re.2005-1943, I

Vought OS2U-1-1940, USA

Grumman 12F-4-1940, USA

58

Cessna AT-8-1940, USA

Grumman F4F-3-1940, USA

Bell P-39-1941, USA

Republic P-43-1941, USA

Consolidated PBY-5-Catalina-1941, USA

Consolidated PB2Y-3-Coronado-1941, USA

Vultee A-35-1942, USA

Douglas A-20-1942, USA

Martin PBM-3 1942, USA

Lockheed PV-I-1942, USA

Boeing B-17G-1942, USA

Curtiss P-40D-1942, USA

Curtiss P-40F Warhawk-1942, USA

Martin B-26-1943, USA

Republic P-47-1943, USA

Vought F4U-1943, USA

North American P-51-1943, USA

North American A-36-1943, USA

Bell P-59-1944, USA

Bell P-63-1944, USA

Northrop P-61-1944, USA

Curtiss C-46-1944, USA

Lockheed P-38-1944, USA

North American B-25J-1944, USA

SAAB 18A-1944, S

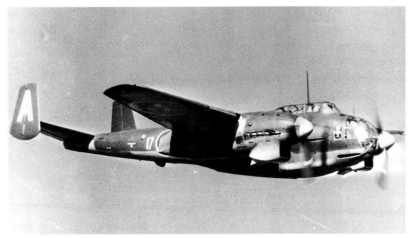

Saab T18-B-1944, S

Tupolev SB-2-1936, USSR

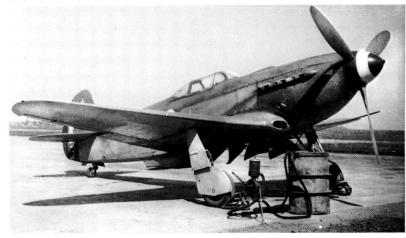

Yakovlev Yak-3-1944, USSR

Mitsubishi Ki-21-II-1941, J

Polikarpov I-16-1937, USSR

Yokosuka D4Y2-1943, J

Kawanishi N1K1 Shiden-1943, J

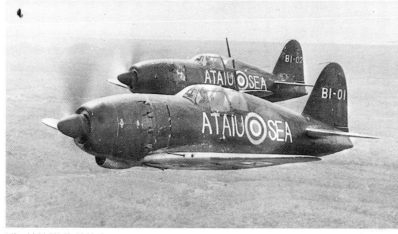

Mitsubishi J2M2-1943, J

Kawanishi N1K Kyofu-1943, J

Nakajima Ki-44-II Shoki-1943, J

Kawanishi H8K2-1943, J